Mary Noailles Murfree

The story of Keedon bluffs

Mary Noailles Murfree

The story of Keedon bluffs

ISBN/EAN: 9783337820961

Printed in Europe, USA, Canada, Australia, Japan

Cover: Foto ©ninafisch / pixelio.de

More available books at **www.hansebooks.com**

THE

STORY OF KEEDON BLUFFS

BY

CHARLES EGBERT CRADDOCK

AUTHOR OF "IN THE CLOUDS," "DOWN THE RAVINE," "IN THE
TENNESSEE MOUNTAINS," "THE PROPHET OF THE
GREAT SMOKY MOUNTAINS," ETC.

BOSTON AND NEW YORK
HOUGHTON, MIFFLIN AND COMPANY
The Riverside Press, Cambridge
1888

THE STORY OF KEEDON BLUFFS.

I.

TOWERING into the air, reflected deep in the river, the great height of Keedon Bluffs is doubled to the casual glance and augmented in popular rumor. Nevertheless a vast mass of rock it is, splintered and creviced, and with rugged, beetling ledges, all atilt, and here and there a niche which holds a hardy shrub, subsisting surely on the bounty of the air or the smile of the sun, for scant sustenance can be coaxed from the solid sandstone.

Here bats and lizards colonize, and amongst the trailing vines winged songsters find a home, and sometimes stealthy, four-footed, marauding shadows, famous climbers, creep in and out of the hollows of the rocks, for it is in the very heart of the wilderness on a slope of the Great Smoky Range. Naught

There sat all day beside the wood-fire a man of middle age, but with a face strangely young. It was like the face of a faded painting, changing only in the loss of color. The hair, growing off a broad forehead, was bleaching fast; the tints had become dim on cheek and lip, but time and care had drawn no lines, and an expression of childlike tranquillity hovered about the downcast eyes, forever shielded by the drooping lids. Life seemed to have ended for him twenty years before, on a day surcharged with disaster, when the great gun, which had been a sort of Thor to him, and which he had served with an admiring affection and reverent care, was spiked by its own cannoneers that it might fall useless into the hands of the enemy. It was the last thing he ever saw — this great silenced god of thunder — as he stood beside it with the sponge-staff in his hand. For among the shells shrieking through the smoky air, one was laden with his doom. A hiss close at hand, the din of an abrupt explosion, and he fell unconscious under the carriage of the piece, and there he was captured.

And when the war was over and he came forth alike from the prison and the hospital, blinded and helpless, naught remained to him but to vaguely ponder on what had been in the days that had gone forever, for he hardly seemed to look to the future, and the present was empty-handed.

He had met his grief and the darkness with a stoicism difficult to comprehend. He spent his days in calm unimbittered meditation, not gentle, but with flashes of his old spirit to attest his unchanged identity. Acclimated to sorrow, without hope, or fear, or anxiety, or participation in life, time could but pass him by, and youth seemed to abide with him.

The old martial interest flared up when Ike told of his discovery on the ledge of Keedon Bluffs.

"What kind o' ball, Ike?" he demanded.

But Ike had been born too late to be discerning as to warlike projectiles.

"I wisht I could lay my hand on it!" said the blind artillery-man. "I'll be bound I'd know, ef I jes' could heft it wunst! Whar did it lodge, Ike? Could I make out ter git a-nigh it? Could ye an' me git thar ter-gether?"

"Ye 'pear b'reft, Abner!" aunt Jemima cried out angrily. "Ye mus' hev los' more 'n yer sight. Hev ye furgot how Keedon Bluffs look? Thar ain't nobody sca'cely ez could keep foot-hold 'mongst them sheer cliffs. An' ye ought n't ter be aggin' on Ike ter climb sech places — git his neck bruk. Ye hain't got no call, sure, ter set store on no mo' cannon-balls, an' artillery, an' sech. I 'low ez ye 'd hev hed enough o' guns, an' I wish ye 'd never hed nuthin' ter do with no rebels."

For this was one of the divided families so usual in East Tennessee, and while the elders had clung to the traditions of their fathers — the men fighting staunchly for the Union — the youngest had as a mere boy fled from his home to join the Confederate forces, and had stood by his gun through many a fiery hail of battle storms. But the bitterness of these differences was fast dying out.

"I hev gin the word," said Ike's father,

and grizzled, and stern, and gigantic, he looked eminently fitted to maintain his behests, "ez no mo' politics air ter be talked roun' this ha'th-stone, Jemimy."

"I ain't talkin' no politics," retorted aunt Jemima, sharply. "But I ain't goin' ter hold my jaw tee-totally. I never kin git over hevin' Ab settin' up hyar plumb benighted! plumb benighted! — ez blind ez a mole!" She shook her head with a sort of acrimonious melancholy.

"Yes," drawlingly admitted the blind artillery-man, all unmoved by this uncheerful discourse. "Yes, that's a true word." He lifted his head suddenly and tossed back the gray hair from his boyish face. "But I *hev* seen — sights!"

Even less tolerated than politics were Ike's repinings and longings for some flaunting military exploit. "Take yer axe," his soldier-father said sternly, "an' show what sort 'n grit ye hev got at the wood-pile."

The blind man with a laugh more leniently suggested, "Ye would n't hev been much use ter we-uns in our battery, Ike, throwin' up a yearth-work ter pertect the guns an' sech, seein' the way ye fairly *de*-spise a spade."

Ike had yet to learn that it is the spirit in which a deed is done that dignifies and magnifies it.

He found the stories of the military glories he would have achieved, had the opportunity fallen to his lot, much more gently treated by a certain young neighbor, who had indeed a good and willing pair of ears, and much readiness and adaptability of assent. Very pliable, withal, was "Skimpy" Sawyer — by the nickname "Skimpy" he was familiarly known, a tribute to his extreme spareness. He was peculiarly thin, and wiry, and loose-jointed. He had a good-natured freckled face, paler for the contrast with a crop of red hair; a twinkling and beguiling brown eye; great nimbleness of limb; and many comical twists of countenance at command.

He accompanied Ike blithely enough to Keedon Bluffs, one afternoon, to look at the cannon-ball on the ledge. A bridle-path, almost a road it might have seemed — for the woods, bereft of undergrowth by the annual conflagrations, gave it space — wound along the side of the mountain near the verge of the cliffs. The river, all scarlet, and silver, and glinting blue, was swirling far down in the chasm beneath them; the sheer sandstone bank rose opposite, solid as a wall; and beyond, the cove — its woods, and cabins, and roads, and fences, bounded by the interlacing mountains — lay spread out like an open map.

Peaceful enough it was to-day, as the boys stood on the Bluffs. There were wings, homeward bound, hurrying through the air, instead of shells with fuses burning bright against the sunset sky. No bugle sang. The river was murmuring low a plaintive minor lay that one might hear forever and never tire. Scanty shrubs of dogwood and sourwood flaunted, red and orange, from the rifts of the great crags; here and there were fissures, irregularly shaped, and dark, save that upon the upper arch of each a ceaseless silvery light shimmered, reflected from the water. On one of the many ledges the cannonball lay unstirred.

"Skimpy, I b'lieve I could actially climb down this hyar bluff an' coon it roun' that thar ledge an' git that ball," said Ike, balancing himself dangerously over the precipice.

So far did it overhang the river at this point that he was startled by seeing a hat and face suddenly looking up at him from the depths below, and it was a moment before he realized that the hat and face were his own, mirrored in a dark pool.

"Ye couldn't climb up ag'in with it in yer paw," retorted Skimpy.

"Naw," Ike admitted. "But ennyhow I'd like ter climb down thar an' see what's in them hollows. I b'lieve I could git inter one o' 'em."

Skimpy had taken a handful of pebbles and was skipping them down the river. He turned so suddenly that the one in his hand flew wide of the mark and nearly tipped his friend's hat off his head.

"What air ye a-hankerin' ter git in one o' them holes fur?" he demanded, surprised, "so ez ye can't git out ag'in? 'Pears-like ter me they'd be a mighty tight fit on sech a big corn-fed shoat ez ye air. An' then I'd hev ter climb down thar an' break my neck, I reckon, ter pull ye out by the heels."

"I wouldn't git in 'thout thar 'peared ter be plenty o' elbow room," Ike qualified.

"Who's that?" said Skimpy, suddenly.

So absorbed had they been that until this moment they were not aware of a slow approach along the road behind them. The sight of a stranger was unusual, but so little curiosity do the mountaineers manifest in unknown passers-by that if the man's manner had had no appeal to the boys, they would hardly have lifted their eyes; they would not even have stared after his back was turned.

But the stranger was about to hail them. He had already lifted his hand with an awkward wave of salutation. Still he fixed his eyes upon them and did not speak as he slouched toward them, and the two boys were impressed with the conviction that he had heard every word that they had been saying.

He was a tall, dawdling fellow of forty, perhaps, carrying a rifle on his shoulder, and dressed in an old brown jeans suit, ill-mended and patched here and there, and with some rents not patched at all. His hair, long and brown, streaked with gray, hung down to his collar beneath his old broad-brimmed wool hat. His face was lined and cadaverous, his features were sharp and shrewd. His eyes, bright, small, dark, and somehow not reassuring, expressed a sort of anxiety and anger that the boys could not comprehend.

There came along the road after him, plainly defined on the summit of the great bluffs, between the woods and the sunset sky, with the river in the abyss beneath and a gleaming star in the haze above, a grotesque little cart, the wheels creaking dismally with every revolution and filling the air with the odor of tar and wagon grease. A lean scraggy ox was between the shafts; a cow shambled along at the tail-board; a calf and two or three dogs trotted further in the rear. The man was moving, evidently, for the poverty-stricken aspect of the vehicle was accented by the meagre show of household utensils — frying-pan, oven, skillet, spinning-wheel — and the bedding, and two or three chairs with which it was laden. On top of it all, sitting in a snug nest of quilts, with a wealth of long yellow hair, tousled and curling upon her shoulders, was a little girl, four or five years old. Her infantile beauty had naught in common with his down-looking, doubtful, careworn face, but she fixed the two boys with a pair of grave, urgent, warning gray eyes, which intimated that whatever the man might do or say he had a small but earnest backer. And though the autumn leaves were red and yellow above her head, the roses of spring bloomed on her cheek, and its sunshine was tangled in her hair; all its buoyant joys were in her laugh when she chose to be merry, and her smile brightened the world for him and for her. She was at the threshold of her life — likely to be a poor thing enough and hedged with limitations, but it had space for all the throbs of living, for all there is of bliss and woe.

The man glanced back at her as he spoke.

"Jes' set a-top thar, Rosamondy; set right still an' stiddy, leetle darter. I hev got a word or two ter pass with these folkses.

Howdy! Howdy! Strangers! Do you-uns know whar old man Binwell hev moved ter hyar-abouts? I stopped at his house a piece back, an' thar war n't nobody thar, 'pears like; chimbly tore down; nare door in the cabin; empty."

He had a strained rasping voice; his tone was not far from tears.

The two boys looked at one another. "Old man Binwell" was Ancient History to them — like Cæsar or Hannibal to boys of wider culture.

"Him? he's dead," they said together, slowly producing the recollection.

"I war 'feared so," said the stranger. "An' whar's 'Liza Binwell, an' Aleck?"

These were more modern. "Waal — her," said Ike, "I hev hearn tell ez how she merried a man ez kem hyar in the war-times along o' the Texas Rangers; an' he seen her then, an' kem arter her when the fightin' war over. I disremember his name. An' he persuaded Aleck an' his fambly ter move with them ter Texas."

The man nodded his head in melancholy reception of the facts.

"They be my brother an' sister," he said drearily. "I hain't hearn nothin' 'bout'n 'em fur a long time. But when we-uns lef' cousin Zeke Tynes's this mornin'— we bided thar las' night— an' started fur Tanglefoot Cove, he 'lowed they war hyar yit. I counted on stayin' with 'em this winter. Who's a-livin' hyar-abouts now ez mought be minded ter let us bide with 'em fur ter-night?"

The boys prompting each other, mentioned the names of the few families in the cove. The stranger's face fell as he listened. There was no house nearer than three or four miles, and the gaunt and forlorn old ox was not a beast of unrivaled speed. The man looked up doubtfully at the ragged edges of a black cloud, barely showing above the mountain summits, but definitely in motion before a wind that was beginning to surge in the upper regions of the air, although it hardly swayed the tops of the trees on Keedon Bluffs. The evening had stormy premonitions, despite the exquisite clearness of the western sky.

"I'm 'feared I'll hev ter feed an' water

the beastis, else he won't hold out so fur," he half soliloquized, looking at the ox, drowsing between the shafts.

Then his attention reverted to the boys.

"Thanky, strangers, thanky fur tellin' me. I dunno ye, ye see, but I war born an' bred hyar-abouts. Thanky. If thar's enny favior I kin do fur you-uns lemme know. Fishin'?" he inquired suddenly.

Skimpy colored. To be asked if he were fishing from the great heights of Keedon Bluffs savored of ridicule.

"How could we fish from sech a place ez this?" he said a trifle gruffly.

"Sure enough! Sure enough! I hed furgot how high 't war," and the stranger came up and peered with them over the river. "I ain't seen this spot fur a good many seasons, folkses," he said, his eyes fixed upon the cavities of the great cliffs across the bend. The cow was munching the half-withered grass by the roadside; the dogs laid their tired bones down among the fallen leaves and went to sleep; Rosamond on her throne among the household goods sat in the red after-glow of

THE STORY OF KEEDON BLUFFS. 17

the sunset, all flushed and gilded, and swung one plump bare foot, protruding its pink dimples from beneath her blue checked homespun dress, and planted the other foot recklessly upon her discarded dappled calico sunbonnet which she suffered to lie among the quilts.

"I tell ye what," he added, still looking about at the darkling forests, at the swift current below the stern grim cliffs, at the continuous shifting shimmer reflected upon the upper arch of the hollows, "you-uns hev got mo' resky 'n ever I be, ter bide 'roun' this hyar spot when it begins ter be cleverly dark."

Both boys looked quickly at him.

"Hain't ye hearn what the old folks tells 'bout them hollows in the rock?"

"Naw!" they exclaimed together.

Skimpy's eyes were distended. He felt a sudden chilly thrill. Ike, although as superstitious as Skimpy, experienced an incredulity before he even heard what this man had to say.

"Waal," resumed the stranger, and he lowered his voice, "the old folks 'low ez the witches lie thar in the daytime — ye know they never die — an' the yearth grants 'em no other place in the day, so they takes ter the hollows in the rock. An' thar they keeps comp'ny with sech harnts ez air minded fur harm ter humans — folks ez hev been hung an' sech. An' then in the evenin'-time they all swarms out tergether."

Skimpy glanced over his shoulder. It was doubtless his fancy, but the foolish boy thought he saw a black head thrust suddenly out of one of the hollows and as suddenly withdrawn.

Now Skimpy was afraid of nothing that went about in the daytime, and indeed of nothing human and mortal. Witches, however, were, he felt, of doubtful destiny and origin, malevolent in character, and he had a vaguely frightful idea concerning their physiognomy and form. He revolted at the prospect of a closer acquaintance.

"Kem on, Ike," he said hastily, clutching his friend's sleeve, "let's go home." And he peered fearfully about in the closing dusk.

But Ike was steadily studying the stranger's face, and the man looked at him though he addressed Skimpy.

"Yes; it's better ter be away from hyar betimes. They air special active in the full o' the moon."

It had risen before the sun had set, and ever and again, from fleecy spaces amongst the ranks of the dark clouds, its yellow lustre streamed forth in myriads of fine fibrous lines slanting upon the tumultuous palpitating purple vapors massed about it. Sometimes a rift disclosed its full splendor as it rode supreme in the midst of the legions of the storm.

"But them witches an' sech air in them holes all day an' ef ennybody war sech a fool ez ter go meddlin' with 'em, ef so be they could git down thar ennywise — *they 'd ketch it!*"

He shook his head in a way that promised horrors.

"What would they do ter 'em?" asked the morbidly fascinated Skimpy. He dared not look over his shoulder now.

The narrator was forced to specify, "Strangle 'em."

Skimpy shuddered, but Ike was ready to laugh outright. He stared at the speaker as if he found him far more queer than his story.

"Ye 'member old man Hobbs?" said the stranger suddenly.

"I hearn my dad tell 'bout'n him," returned Ike. "Old man Hobbs said he walked off'n the Bluffs through bein' drunk an' fell inter the river — though ez he war picked up alive folks b'lieved he never fell off'n the Bluffs, but jes' said so, bein' drunk an' foolish."

"Naw, it's a fac'," said the stranger, as if he knew all about it. "The witches got ter clawin' an' draggin' of him, an' they drug him in the water, bein' ez he war a-foolin' roun' them hollows an' this hyar spot ginerally."

"Oh, I'm goin'," cried Skimpy; then as he started off, the idea of being alone in the great woods, with the night settling down, came upon him with overwhelming terror, and he renewed his pleas to Ike. "Kem on, Ike. We-uns hev been hyar long enough."

"Oh, shet up," cried Ike roughly. "The witches ain't goin' ter strangle ye ez long ez ye hev got me alongside ter pertect ye."

He wanted to hear more of what this man had to say, for he placed a different interpretation upon his words. But Rosamond had lifted her voice, and seeing that her father was preparing to start anew on their forlorn journeying was insisting on a change in the arrangement.

"I wants ye ter let the calf ride!" she cried in her vibrating musical treble. "I wants the calf ter ri-ride!"

The calf added its voice to hers, and bleated as it ran along behind. It had evidently come far and was travel-worn.

"I wants the calf ter ride wif *me!*" she cried again, with an imperious squeal upon the last syllable.

"The calf can't ride, Rosamondy," the man said, in gentlest expostulation. "He's too heavy fur the steer — pore steer."

"Naw, pore calf!" cried Rosamondy, and burst into tearful rage.

"Ah, Rosamondy, ain't ye 'shamed ter be

sech a bad leetle gal? Ain't ye 'feared them boys 'll go off an' tell ev'ybody what a bad leetle gal ye be!"

But Rosamond evidently did not care how far and wide they published her "badness," and after the boys had turned off into the woods, leaving the wagon creaking along the road with the ox between the shafts, and the man driving the cow in advance, they still heard the piteous bleats of the little calf trotting behind, and Rosamondy's insistent squeal, "I wants the calf ter ride wif *me!*"

In the dense woods the darkness was deeper; indeed they might only know that as yet it was not night by seeing vaguely the burly forms of the great boles close at hand. The shadowy interlacing boughs above their heads merged indistinguishably into the mass of foliage. Every sound was startlingly loud and in the nature of an interruption of some sylvan meditation. The rustle of their feet in the crisp fallen leaves seemed peculiarly sibilant, and more than once suggested a pursuer. Skimpy looked hastily over his shoulder, — only the closing obscurity that baffled his vision. A gust of wind swept through the woods rousing a thousand weird utterances of bough, and leaf, and rock, and hollow, and died away again into the solemn silence.

Skimpy quickened his pace. "Kem on, Ike," he muttered, and started at the sound of his own voice.

Suddenly Ike Guyther, without a word of warning, turned about and began to retrace his way.

"Whar ye bound fur?" cried Skimpy, laying hold on his arm and striving to keep him back.

"Bound fur the Bluffs," said Ike. "'T won't take we-uns long. I jes' wanter sati'fy myself whether that thar man air too 'feard o' witches ter water an' feed his steer at that thar spring 'mongst the rocks nigh Keedon Bluffs."

"*We-uns!*" cried Skimpy. "I tell ye now, I'd be palsied in every toe an' toe-nail too 'fore I'd go a inch."

"Waal, I'll ketch up with ye," said Ike.

Skimpy made an effort to hold him, but

the stronger boy pulled easily away from him and ran. A whirl of the dry leaves, a whisking sound, and he was lost among the trees.

He did not keep this speed. He had slackened his pace to a walk before he emerged upon the road that ran between the verge of the bluffs and the woods. It seemed much earlier now, for here was presented the definite aspect of the evening instead of the uncertain twilight of the forest. In the faint blue regions of the zenith still loitered gauzy roseate reflections of the gorgeous sunset, not yet overspread by the black cloud gradually advancing up the vast spaces of the heavens. The river, in its cliff-bound channel, caught here and there a glittering moonbeam on its lustrous dark current. The amber tints of the western sky shaded into a pallid green above the duskily purple mountains. A pearl-colored mist, most vaguely visible, lurked in the depths of the cove.

Suddenly the rocks by the roadside stood distinct and ruddy in a broad flickering red flare; there were moving figures, grotesque elongated shadows, among the trees. Ike Guyther stopped short, with a sudden dread of the witches of Keedon Bluffs trembling within him. Then, for he was stout-hearted, he ventured to creep along a few steps further. There under the boughs of the pines and the scarlet oaks and the yellow hickory trees a fire of pine knots flamed, throwing hilarious sparks and frisking smoke high into the melancholy white mists gathering in the woods; and grouped about it — not witches nor harnts — but the humble travelers eating their supper by the wayside. Ike recognized the clumsy cart in the shadowy background; the ox, out of the shafts, now munching his well-earned feed; the cow lying on the ground licking the head of her calf. And sitting by the fire with her yellow hair glittering, her face illumined by the blaze, her pink feet presented to the warmth, was Rosamondy, commenting gravely as her father broiled a bit of bacon on the coals and deftly constructed an ash-cake. The dogs too sat beside the fire, all upright and wide awake, and with an alert interest in the proceedings. Now and then as the man turned the meat and the savory odor would rise, one of them would twist his head admiringly askew and lick his chops in anticipation.

The little girl talked continuously, her babyish voice clear on the still air, and the man listened and affected amazement when she thought she was astonishing him, and laughed mightily when she laughed, and agreed punctiliously with whatever she might say. But indeed she seemed a person who would tolerate little contradiction.

The picture vanished suddenly as Ike Guyther turned back into the sombre depths of the woods.

"Waal, sir!" said the shrewd young fellow to himself, "whoever b'lieves ez witches an' harnts swarm out 'n them hollows in the night times ter strangle folks ez be nigh by, the man ez stops ter cook his supper a-top o' the Bluffs — don't. An' that air a true word."

The more he reflected upon the circumstance, as he took his way through the woods to rejoin Skimpy, the more he felt sure that this stranger had overheard his proposal to climb down to those hollows, and had some purpose to serve in frightening him away from the cavities in the cliffs.

Still pondering upon this mystery he looked back once after he and Skimpy had reached the levels of Tanglefoot Cove. The advancing cloud still surged over the summit of the range, throwing its darkling shadows far down the steeps. In the mingled light of the dying day and the fitful gleam of the moon he could yet distinguish the stern grim crags, and below, on the slope where the grassy road wound in serpentine convolutions, he saw the cart with the little girl once more perched high, the ox between the shafts, the man driving the cow, the dogs and the calf trotting in the rear — all the little procession on the way again to seek shelter in some hospitable farmer's cabin. And thus they fared down the rugged mountain ways into the future of Tanglefoot Cove.

II.

When clouds gather over Tanglefoot Cove, and storms burst on the mountain slopes, the sounds of the tempest are redoubled by the echoes of the crags, trumpeting anew the challenge of the wind and reiterating the slogan of the thunder. For begirt on every side by clifty ranges the secluded valley lies. Ike's mother, listening to the turmoil of the powers of the air and the sinister response of the powers of the earth, as the surly night closed in, waited with anxiety for the boy's return, and welcomed him with a brightening face as he entered.

A great fire flared on the hearth, illumining the ill-laid puncheon floor; the high bed with its gayly tinted quilts; the warping bars; the spinning-wheel; the guns upon their racks of deer-antlers; the strings of red peppers, swaying overhead; the ladder leading up to the shadowy regions of the roof-room through a black hole in the ceiling. The fire-light even revealed in a dusky nook a rude box on rockers — which had cradled in turn these stalwart soldiers, and later Ike, himself — and, under a low shelf in the corner, a tiny empty chair.

The wind rushed down the chimney, and every cranny piped a shrill fife-like note, and the thunder rolled.

"I dunno when I ever hev seen sech a onexpected storm," said Ike's father as he hung up the ox-yoke on the wall, having turned out the team from his wagon.

"T' wouldn't s'prise me none," said aunt Jemima, "ef 't war jes' a big blow ez tore down the fodder-stack an' rooted up yer orcherd' an' never gin ye nare drop o' rain fur the drought;" she cast an almost reprehensive glance upon him, as if it were through his neglect that he was threatened with these elemental disasters.

"Waal," he retorted, "I ain't settin' myself ter fault the Lord's weather. An' my immortal hopes ain't anchored in a fodder-stack, nuther in the orcherd. An' thar's no dispensation ez kin happen ez I ain't in an' about able ter stan'."

Even aunt Jemima was rather taken aback by this sturdy defiance of fate. She had nothing to say, which was rather rare, for she had given most of her declining years to argument, and much practice had developed her natural resources of contradiction, which were originally great. As Ike's father was himself testy and dogmatic, and the blind man often proclaimed that he took "nuthin' off'n nobody," the family might have been divided by dissension were it not for the placid temperament of Ike's mother. She received no credit, however, for — as people often observed — she was not born a Guyther and had "no call to be high-strung an' sperited." She had been a great beauty in her girlhood and had had lovers by the score, but care and age and poverty had bereft her of her personal charms, and she had neither culture nor grace of manner to fill the breach. Her hard experience of life, however, had failed to sour her temper, and her placidity had something of the buoyancy of youth, as she often declared, "It'll be all the same a hundred year from now."

"'Pears like ter me 't won't blow that hard," she remarked as she stirred the corn-meal batter in a wooden bowl, "the wind don't fool much with our orcherd nohow."

"I'd ruther hev the wind 'n, no rain," said aunt Jemima, plaintively.

"I'm a-thinkin' we'll git rain too, jes' 'bout enough. Yellimints don't neglec' us noways ez I kin see. Seedtime an' harvest shell never fail"—

"Kems mighty nigh it, wunst in a while," said aunt Jemima, shaking her head. "Ef ye hed enny jedgment an' forecast, M'ria, ye'd look fur troubles ahead like them ye hev seen."

There was a shadow on the wasted placid face under Mrs. Guyther's sunbonnet as she knelt to put the potatoes with their jackets on in the ashes to roast.

"Waal — let troubles go down the road. I wouldn't hev liked thar looks no better through viewin' 'em 'fore I got ter 'em. I ain't a-goin' ter turn roun' now ter see ag'in how awful they war whenst they war a-facin' me. Let troubles go down the road."

And so she covered the potatoes while aunt Jemima knit off another row.

The next moment both were besprinkled with ashes; the chimney-place seemed full of a vivid white light never kindled on a hearth-stone; there was a frightful crack of thunder, then it seemed to roll upon the roof, and the cabin rocked with the fierce assaults of the wind.

"That thar shot war aimed p'int blank," said the blind artillery-man, thrusting his hands deeper in his pockets, and stretching out his long legs, booted to the knee. His gray hair had flakes of the white ashes scattered upon it.

"Suthin' mus' hev been struck right hyar in the door-yard," said aunt Jemima. She had laid down her knitting with a sort of affronted and expostulatory air. "I'll be bound it's the martin-house."

"I'll be bound it's nuthin' we want," said Mrs. Guyther.

There was a hesitating drop, another, upon the clap-boards that roofed the house; then came the heavy down-pour of the rain, the renewed gusts of the wind, and amidst it all a husky cry.

They turned and looked at one another. Then Hiram Guyther lifted the latch. The opening door let in the moist, melancholy air of the stormy evening that seemed to saturate the room in pervading it. A crouching figure, the sombre clouds, the slanting lines of rain, the tossing dark woods, were barely visible without, until a sudden, blue forked flash of lightning played through this dusky landscape of grays and browns. As it broadened into a diffusive red flare, it showed an ox with low-hanging horns between the shafts of a queer little cart, piled high with household goods. Among them half smothered in the quilts — wound tightly about her shoulders — appeared the yellow head, and pink face, and big, startled gray eyes of a little girl. It was only for a moment that this picture was presented, then it faded away to the dark monotony of the shapeless shadows of the woods; and as

Ike went to the door he heard the drawling voice of the man he had seen at Keedon Bluffs asking Hiram Guyther for shelter for the night.

"We-uns hev been travelin' an' hoped ter git settled fur the winter 'fore enny sech weather ez this lit onto us."

"Kem in, traveler! Ye air hearty welcome ef ye kin put up with sech ez we-uns kin gin ye," the hospitable mountaineer drawled sonorously, raising his voice that it might be heard above the blast.

"We'll all hev pleurisy, though, ef ye don't shet that thar door, an' keep it shet," muttered aunt Jemima, in her half articulate undertone.

She was silent the next moment, for there was slowly coming into the room — nay, into the grim heart of aunt Jemima — a new power in her life. A yellow-topped, cylindrical bundle, much like a silking ear of corn, was set on end in the middle of the puncheon floor, and as the strange man unwrapped the parti-colored quilts from about it, there stepped forth, golden-haired, ragged, smiling, with one finger between her small and jagged teeth, with dimples that graced the poverty and atoned for the dirt, a little girl, looking quaintly askance at the group about the fire, and making straight for the little chair under the shelf. She did not move it. She sat there, under the shelf, smiling and pink and affectedly shy.

Aunt Jemima stared over her spectacles. She too smiled as her eyes met the child's — a grim demonstration. Her features adapted themselves to it reluctantly as if they were not used to it.

"Kem up by the fire, child," she said.

But the little girl sat still under the shelf.

"Warm yer feet!" aunt Jemima further sought to beguile her.

The little guest's pleased smile took on the proportions of an ecstatic grin, but she only settled herself more comfortably in the small chair under the shelf.

Aunt Jemima, tall, bent, raw-boned, rose and approached the little girl with a seriousness that might have seemed formidable. She looked up with her big gray eyes all shining in the firelight, but did not offer to retreat. She only clutched fast the arms of the little chair that had taken her delighted fancy, and since she evidently would not leave it for a moment, the old woman pulled the chair, child and all, in front of the fire, into the full genial radiance of the blazing hickory logs. Ike and his mother and the hounds looked on at this proceeding, and one of the dogs, following close after the chair when it was dragged over the floor, squeaked in a low-spirited key and wheezed and licked aunt Jemima's hand, as it grasped the knob, seeking to call attention to himself. "Now ain't ye a nice one, a-goin' on four legs an' switchin' a tail a-hint ye, an' yit ondertakin' ter be ez jealous ez folks," she admonished him, and he frisked a little, glad to be spoken to on any terms, and sat down between her and the little girl, who still clutched the arms of the tiny chair.

"Waal now, it air a plumb shame fur her ter be bar'foot this weather," said aunt Jemima, contemplating the little guest.

The old woman was abashed when she glanced up and saw the child's companion, who, with Hiram Guyther, had just returned from the task of stabling the ox and sheltering the wagon, for she had not intended that the stranger should overhear this reflection.

"I know that," he drawled in a desolate low-spirited cadence, his eyes blinking in the light of a tallow dip that Mrs. Guyther had set on the mantel-piece, and seeking with covert curiosity to distinguish the members of the group. He paused suddenly, for at the sound of his voice the blind man abruptly rose to his feet and stretched out his arms gropingly. "Who — who?" he stuttered, as if his speech were failing him — "who be this ez hev kem hyar ter-night?" He passed his hands angrily across his eyes — "Ain't it Jerry Binwell?"

Blind as he was, he was the first to recognize the newcomer with that sharpening of the remaining senses which seeks to compensate for the loss of one. But indeed Jerry Binwell had outwardly changed beyond recognition in the twenty years since they had last seen him, when he and Abner were mere boys in the Cove, and had run off together to join the Southern army.

Binwell took a step toward the door as if he regretted his entrance and wished that he still might go.

"What hev gin ye the insurance ter kem a-nigh me!" Abner cried angrily, still reaching out with hands that were far enough from what they sought to clutch. The child, in her little chair at his feet, gazed up with awe. "Arter all ye done in camp, a-lyin' an' a-deludin' me; an' then slanderin' an' backbitin' me ter the off 'cers, an' men; an' every leetle caper I cut, gittin' me laid by the heels fur it; an' ev'ry time ye got in a scrape, puttin' the blame on me. An' at last — at last " — he cried, raising his voice and smiting his hands together as if overborne anew by the despair and scorn of it, " whenst we war flanked by the Feds ye deserted! An' ye gin 'em the word how ter surround our battery! An' cannon, an' cannoneers, an' horses, an' caissons, an' battery-wagon, all war captured! That war yer sheer o' the fight."

He paused for a moment. Then he took a step forward, his stalwart, soldierly figure erect, his face flushed, his hand pointing toward the door.

"G 'long!" he said roughly. "Go out. Haffen o' this house is mine. An' ye sha'n't bide in it one minute. I hev hed enough of ye an' yer ways. Go out!"

"It's a plumb harricane out'n doors, Ab," Mrs. Guyther pleaded timidly. "Won't ye — won't ye jes' let him bide till the storm's over?"

III.

THE lightning flashed; the thunder pealed. The blind man lifted his head, listening. He hesitated between his righteous scorn, his sense of injury, and the hospitality that was the instinct of his nature. He yielded at last, shamefacedly, as to a weakness.

"Waal, waal," he said, in an off-hand cavalier fashion, "keep Jerry dry; he's mighty val'y'ble. Good men air sca'ce, Jerry; take keer o' yerse'f!"

He laughed sarcastically and resumed his chair. As he did so his booted knee struck against the little girl, still staring at him with eyes full of wonder.

"What's this?" he cried sharply, his nerves jarring yet with the excitement. He had not before noticed her. "I can't see!" with a shrill rising inflection, as if the affliction were newly realized.

A propitiatory smile broke upon her face.

"Jes' Rosamondy." Her voice vibrated through the room — the high quavering treble of childhood that might have been shrill were it not so sweet.

"Jerry's leetle gal," said aunt Jemima.

"Shucks!" he exclaimed, contemptuously, and turned aside.

"Set down, Rosamondy," said aunt Jemima, assuming a grandmotherly authority. "Set down like a good leetle gal."

But Rosamond was not amenable to bidding and paid no heed. She had risen from her chair and stood by the side of the blind artillery-man.

"Set down," aunt Jemima admonished her again. "*He* can't see."

"Kin ye feel?" she said, suddenly laying her dimpled pink hand upon his. She gazed up at him, her eyes bright and soft, her lips parted, her cheek flushed. "Kin ye feel my hand?"

He looked surly, affronted for a moment. He shook the light hand from his own. It fell upon his knee where Rosamond leaned her weight upon it. There was a subtle change on his face. In his old debonair way he drawled, "Yes, I kin feel. What's this?"—he laid his hand upon her hair—"Flax, I reckon. Hyar, Sis' Jemimy, hyar's that flax ye war goin' ter hackle. Mus' I han' it over ter ye?"

He made a feint of lifting her by her hair, and she sank down beside him, screaming with laughter till the rafters rang.

Aunt Jemima had taken the sock from her knitting needles and was swiftly putting on the stitches for newly projected work.

"Lemme medjure ye fur a stockin'," she said, reaching out for the little girl. "Look at the stitches this child's stockin' will take! The fatness of her is s'prisin'. An' ef Ab air willin'," she continued, "I want Rosamondy ter bide hyar till I can knit her a couple o' pair o' stockin's an' mend up her clothes."

"I dunno 'bout'n that," said Jerry Binwell. He had seated himself in a chair, his garments dripping with rain, and small puddles forming from them on the floor. "I dunno ez we-uns kin bide enny arter the rain 's over."

The capable aunt Jemima cast upon him a glance which seemed to contrast his limp, forlorn, and ineffective personality with her own stalwart moral value.

"I ain't talkin' ter you-uns, Jerry, nor thinkin' 'bout ye, nuther," she remarked slightingly. "I done said my say," she continued after the manner of a proclamation. "That thar child air goin' ter bide hyar till I fix her clothes comfortable — ef it takes me a year." Then with a recollection of her brother's grievance she again added, "Ef Ab's willin'."

The stocking was already showing a ribbed top of an admirable circumference. Aunt Jemima evidently felt a pride in its proportions which was hardly decorous.

Jerry made no reply. He looked disconsolately at the fire from under the brim of his rain-soaked hat, that now and then contributed a drop to his cheek, which thus bore a tearful aspect. Presently he broke the silence, speaking in a strained rasping voice.

"Ef I hed knowed ez Ab held sech a pack o' old gredges ag'in me I would n't kem nigh hyar," — he glanced at the stalwart soldierly form bending to the little laughing maiden. "Ab dunno what I tole the en'my — he warn't thar. I never tole the en'my nuthin'. An' ennybody ez be captured kin be accused o' desertin' — ef folks air so minded. I never deserted, nuther. An' sech gredges ez Ab hev got," he continued, complainingly, "air fur what I done, an' what I ain't done whenst I war nuthin' but a boy."

Ab turned his imperious youthful face toward him. "Ye hesh up!" he said. "Thar ain't no truce hyar fur you-uns."

His attention reverted instantly to the babyish sorceress at his knee, who with an untiring repetition and an unfailing delight in the exercises would rise from her chair and gently touch his hand or brow crying out, with a joyous voice full of laughter, "Kin you-uns feel my hand!" Then he would pinch her rosy cheeks and retort in a gruff undertone, "Kin you-uns feel my hand!"

They all behaved, Ike thought, as if they had found something choice and of rare value. And if the truth must be known, he watched the scene with somewhat the same sentiments which animated the old dogs. He shared their sense of supersedure, and he noticed how they whined and could take comfort in no spot about the hearth; how they would walk around three times and lie down with a sigh of renunciation, to get up suddenly with an afflicted wheeze, and hunt about for another place where the distemper of their jealous hearts might let them find rest for their lazy bones. They all sought to intrude themselves upon notice. One of them crept to aunt Jemima and humbly licked her foot, only to have that stout and decided member deal him a prompt rebuke upon the nose, eliciting a yelp altogether out of proportion to the twinge inflicted; for the dog, since he was not going to be petted, was glad to have some grievance to howl about, as he might thus more potently appeal to her sympathy. The hound that was accustomed to lead the blind man was even more insistent in his manifestations. He went and rested his head on his master's knee, while the little girl sat close in her chair on the opposite side, and he wagged his tail and looked imploringly up in the sightless face. But Rosamondy leaned across and patted the dog on the head, and let him take her hand between his teeth, and jovially pulled his ears, and finally caught him by both, when they lost their balance and went over on the hearth together in a wild scramble, about to be "scorched an' scarified ter death," as aunt Jemima said snappishly when she rescued the little girl, who was a very red rose now, and with a tender shake deposited her once more in her chair. Then the old dog left his master, and ran and sat by her and sought to incite more gambols.

But Ike was not so easily reconciled. He did not appreciate the gratulation in this acquisition that pervaded the fireside. She was nothing but a girl, and a little one at that. Girls were not uncommon; in fact they abounded. They were nothing to brag on — Ike was young as yet. They could n't do anything that was worth while. To be sure the miller's daughter *was* tolerably limber, and could walk on the timbers of the race, which were high above the stream. But how she worked her arms above her head to balance herself! And she pretended to shoot once in a while; he would rather be the mark than stand forty yards from it. That was the best he could say for her shooting. And she was the most valuable and desirable specimen of girlhood in his acquaintance. He noted with a sort of wonder that his mother, through sheer absorption, let the hoe-cake burn to a cinder, and had to make up and bake one anew. And when it was at last done, and placed on the table with the platter of venison and corn dodgers, he did not admire particularly the simple but vivid delight with which Rosamond greeted the prospect of supper. But even the saturnine Hiram Guyther looked at her with a smile as she ran glibly around the table, and with her hands on the edge stood on her tiptoes to see what they were to have, and he turned and said to Jerry Binwell, "She air a powerful bouncin' leetle gal. I reckon we-uns 'll hev ter borry her, Jerry — ef," recollecting in his turn that this was the child of his blind brother's enemy, "ef Ab 's willin'."

The dawdling Jerry, still staring disconsolately at the fire, drawled non-committally, "I dunno 'bout'n that."

Despite all her fervor of anticipation, Rosamondy was not hungry. She knelt in her chair at the table to be tall enough to participate in the exercises, and her beaming pink face, and her tossing yellow hair, and her glittering rows of squirrel teeth — she showed a great many of them when she laughed — irradiated the space between aunt Jemima and Ab. Her conduct was what Ike mentally designated as "robustious." She bounced up and down; she fed her supper to the dogs; she let the cat climb up the back of her chair and put two paws on her shoulder among her tangled yellow curls and lap milk out of her saucer. She shrieked and bobbed about till Ike did not know whether he was eating hoe-cake or sawdust. She looked as if she were out in a high wind. Aunt Jemima vainly sought to make her eat her supper, but the displeasure on her face was a feigned rebuke for which Rosamond cared as little as might be. When she concluded her defiance of all those observances, which Ike had been taught to respect, by taking her empty saucer, inverting it and perching it on her tousled yellow pate after the manner of a cap, Hiram Guyther, the meal being ended, caught her up delightedly and rode her to the fireplace on his shoulder.

"I declar', Jerry," he exclaimed cordially, his big bass voice booming amidst the trilling treble laughter, "we-uns 'll hev ter steal this hyar leetle gal from ye."

And Jerry, demurely disconsolate, replied, "I reckon I could n't spare her, right handy."

Presently Ike began to notice that it was very difficult for Rosamondy to get enough of a joke. She refused to descend from the gigantic mountaineer's shoulder, and when he tried to put her down clung to his collar, around his neck, indeed she did not scruple to clutch his hair. Hiram Guyther had not for a long time taken such active exercise — for in this region men of his age assume all the privileges and ailments of advanced years — as during the time that he trotted up and down the floor with the little girl on his shoulder, playing he was a horse. A hard driver he had, to be sure, and he was obliged to stamp, and shy, and jump, and spurt, smartly. He did not look quite sensible Ike thought in unfilial surprise.

The whole domestic routine was upset. His mother and aunt Jemima had left the clearing away of the dishes and applied themselves to pulling out the old trundle-bed — long ago too short for any of the family — and they arranged it with loving care and much precaution against the cold and draughts.

"I'm fairly feared she mought roll out, an' git her spine bruk, or her neck," said aunt Jemima, knitting her wrinkled brows in affectionate alarm as she looked at the trundle-bed that was about two feet from the floor.

"I reckon not," said Jerry meekly as he inoffensively watched the arrangement of the cosy nest. "She never fell off 'n the top o' the kyart — an' sometimes she napped ef the sun war hot."

"An' ye air the only man in Tennessee ez would hev sot the leetle critter up thar — an' her tender bones so easy ter break," said aunt Jemima, tartly.

"Waal, I done the bes' I could fur her," drawled Jerry in his tearful voice, looking harried and woeful.

And remembering how kind and gentle he had seemed to his little daughter, Ike wondered that he did not feel sorry for Jerry when aunt Jemima intimated that he was heedless of her safety and neglected her. But watching the man Ike was even more disapproving of the wholesale adoration which the family seemed disposed to lay at the feet of the little girl and of her adoption into a solicitude and love that was almost parental. He believed that Jerry had an inimical appreciation of all the slighting consideration of him, but offered no objection to the authority they had assumed over Rosamondy, thinking it well that she should get all she could out of them.

Her hilarity seemed to increase as the hour waxed later, and when aunt Jemima finally took her, squirming and wriggling and shouting with laughter, from Hiram Guyther's shoulder and tucked her into the trundle-bed with a red quilt drawn up close under her dimpled white chin and her long yellow hair,

Ike expected to see the whole bed paraphernalia rise up while she resurrected herself.

"Ye lie still, now," said aunt Jemima sternly, laying a hand upon each shoulder.

A vague squirm, a sleepy chuckle, and Rosamond was eclipsed for the night.

"Waal, that beats my time;" said the grim aunt Jemima softly. "Asleep a'ready!"

She sat down and resumed her knitting. Hiram Guyther was mopping his brow with his handkerchief.

"I feel like ez ef I 'd los' ten pound o' flesh," he said. And Ike thought it not unlikely. His mother was washing the dishes; the blind man was reflectively smoking his pipe; the dogs came and disposed themselves with reproachful sighs prominently about the hearth. Jerry Binwell did not share their relief. He stirred uneasily in his chair, the legs grating on the puncheon floor, as if he feared that with this distraction removed the more unfriendly attention of the family might be directed to him. No one spoke for a moment, all listening to the tumult of the rain on the roof; they had not before noticed that the violence of the storm had subsided into a steady downpour. Then, after a glance at the sleeping face, pensive now and ethereal and sensitive, framed in the yellow hair that streamed over the red quilt, aunt Jemima turned a long calculating gaze on Jerry Binwell.

As its result she observed bluntly, " Her mother mus' hev been a mighty pritty woman."

If the inference that Rosamond inherited none of her beauty from her father was apprehended by Jerry, he did not resent it. His eyes filled with tears.

" Yes, she war," he said, dropping his voice to a husky undertone. "She war a plumb beauty whenst she war young, afore she tuk ter ailin'."

Another pause ensued. The rain beat monotonously; the eaves dripped and dripped; the trees on the mountain slopes swayed, and creaked, and crashed together.

"It hev been mighty hard on me," Jerry again lifted up his dreary voice, " ter know how bes' ter keer fur Rosamondy — not bein' a 'oman myself an' sech. I know she's ragged, but I can't mend her clothes so they'll stay; she jumps so onexpected. I can't sew fitten fur much, though I hev tried ter l'arn. I 'pear ter be slow an' don't get much purchase on it. I can't keep no stiddy aim with a needle, nuther. An' all the wimmen ez ever hed a chance at Rosamondy tuk ter quar'lin over her, like them done ez Sol'mon hed ter jedge a-twixt, till I war actually afeared she be tore in two. Ever since the war I hev been livin' down in Persimmon Cove an' thar it war I merried. 'Bout a year ago Em'line she died o' the lung complaint. An' then the 'tother wimmen, her sister an' mother, they quar'led so over Rosamondy, an' set tharse'fs so ter spite me every which-a-way, ez I jes' 'lowed I'd fetch her up hyar fur this winter ter bide with my folks awhile. An' I fund 'em all dead or moved away — jes' my luck! Rosamondy an' me hev hed a mighty hard time. I hev been mighty poor, never could git no good holt on nuthin'. I ain't felt much like tryin' noways sence Em'line lef'; 'pears mighty hard she could n't hev been let ter bide awhile longer." And once more his eyes filled with tears.

"Waal, mournin' the dead is grudgin' 'em the glory," said Mrs. Guyther in her comforting tones.

"I know that," said Jerry, "I hev tried ter bow my mind;" his eyes were still full of tears. And Ike, looking at them, was disposed to wonder where he got them, so little did they seem genuine.

The tallow dip on the mantel-piece went out in a splutter and left them all sitting in the red glow of the fire, which was a mass of coals where the white flames had been. It was far later than the usual bed-time of the family, and thus they were reminded of it. Mrs. Guyther, kneeling on the hearth, began to cover the coals with the plentiful ashes that lay in great heaps on either side. The dogs, summoned by Hiram Guyther to leave the house, pulled themselves into various efforts at an upright posture, and sat gazing blinkingly at the fire with a determination to misunderstand the tenor of his discourse. One of them glanced over his shoulder at the door and shivered at the thought of the bleak dampness outside. Another yawned shrilly and was adjured by aunt Jemima to hesh his mouth — did n't he know he 'd wake the baby up if he kep' yappin' that-a-way.

"Let the dogs alone, Hiram," said Mrs. Guyther, "they count on bein' allowed ter stay till the las' minit. Ye show Jerry whar he hev ter sleep whilst I fix the fire."

After the host had shown Jerry up the ladder to the shadowy roof-room, Abner, who had not again spoken to the visitor, and seeming as if he were gazing ponderingly into the fire, said suddenly to the two women : —

"What do that leetle gal look like?"

Mrs. Guyther paused with the shovel in her hand, as she still knelt on the hearth.

Aunt Jemima dropped her knitting in her lap.

They replied in a breath : —

"The pritties' yearthly human ever you see!"

"Bigges' gray eyes!" cried Mrs. Guyther, "an' black lashes!"

"An' yaller hair — yaller ez gold an' haffen a yard long," exclaimed aunt Jemima.

"Fine bleached skin, white ez milk," said Mrs. Guyther.

"An' yit she's all pink — special when she laughs," cried aunt Jemima, "jes' like these hyar wild roses — ye 'member 'em, don't ye, Ab, growin' in the fence corner in the June weather "—

— "Sech a many of 'em over yander by Keedon Bluffs," put in Mrs. Guyther.

"I 'member 'em," said Ab.

"Jes' the color of 'em when she laughs — jes' like they be, a-blowin' about in the wind," declared aunt Jemima.

"She's named right — Rosy; she's like 'em," said Mrs. Guyther.

The red glow of the embers was full on the blind man's face, encircled by shadows. It seemed half smiling, or perhaps that was some illusion of the fire-light, for it was pensive too, and wistful. He pondered for a while; then — "I'd like ter see her," he said, simply. "I would."

Every word was distinctly audible in the roof-room. Jerry Binwell sat in a rickety chair amongst the shadows, his head attentively bent down, his hands on his knees, his hat drooping half over his face. The rifts between the puncheons of the flooring admitted a red glow from the fire-lit room below, and illumined the dusky loft with longitudinal shafts of light. A triumphant smile played over his face as the women talked of the beauty of the little Rosamond — a smile that might have expressed only paternal pride and satisfaction in the comfortable results of the evening. But when the blind man's rich low voice sounded, "I'd like ter see her — I would," the listener's face changed. The narrow gleam of light from the cracks in the floor played upon the mocking animosity in his eyes, the sneer on his lips as they parted. He stood suddenly erect, in a tense soldierly position — among the shadows, and the bags of "yerbs," and the old clothes, and the peltry hanging from the ridge-pole — brought his heels together with a swift precision, and then the deserter mockingly carried his hand to his hat in a military salute.

"I would," dreamily reiterated the blind soldier in the room below.

The deserter, relaxing his martial attitude to his normal slouch, noiselessly smote his thigh with his right hand, and burst into silent laughter.

IV.

THE next morning Ike woke with an odd, heavy sense of having sustained some serious misfortune, and it was several moments before he could identify it; when he did, he was amazed to find it only his intuitive distrust of the stranger's presence here, and an aversion to its continuance. He upbraided himself in the same instant for the inhospitable thought. "Hyar I be, actially a-grudgin' the houseless ones a shelter from the yellimints," he said in shame.

He was disappointed, however, to observe that after breakfast there was no sign of an impending departure; Jerry Binwell easily adapted himself to the domestic routine and smoked and lounged before the fire, or strolled lazily about the yard. Ike thought, for all he so readily made himself at home, that his sordid, weak, sly face looked strangely alien and out of place among the sterling, honest, candid countenances of the family circle. So ill at ease did Ike feel with this vague anxiety that he was glad enough when his mother bethought herself that she needed logwood from the store. Mounted on the old gray mare he set out on this errand, feeling liberated in a measure, riding against the fresh wind that seemed to blow away the vexing distemper of his thoughts.

The rain had revivified the world; everything seemed made anew. The colors were so luminously clear; how splendidly the maples deployed down the mountain side, with red and amber and purple gleams; every needle of the pines was tipped with a raindrop, prismatically glittering. Mists rose from the intermediate valleys between the ranges, and folded their wings for a space, dallying on the summit, and then, drawn sunwards, lifted with silent ethereal grace into the soft blue sky. How lofty the mountains seemed to-day — how purple! Even the red mud beneath his mare's hoofs had depths of rich ocherous tints, restful to the eye. It splashed monotonously under the steady jogging tread, so muffled that a squirrel, nimbly speeding along the topmost rail of the wayside fence, had no thought of an approach, and seemed a fellow-traveler; a swift one! — the old mare is soon far behind. And now the river is crossed, swollen by the rain and of a clay-color, instead of its wonted limpid silvery tint, and deep enough in the middle to make the old mare flounder to the girth and then unwillingly swim, while Ike gathers himself on his knees on the saddle to keep out of the cold water. And now up the rocky bank in the deep shadowy woods, — where there is no fence on either side of the road, which seems merely a vagrant wheel-track here and there in the mud, covered with the yellow and red and brown fallen leaves — and all the bosky vistas are full of richest color. Everywhere the giant trees close thickly in — no sign of mountains now, save the tonic balsamic air in proof of the altitudes. Only the pines and cedars and the jungles of the laurel are green, and green they will be all winter. Hear that! a fox barks in that dense tangle — are the frost grapes ripe, old Crafty? And suddenly between a scarlet oak and a yellow hickory a section of purple mountain shows, a floating capricious sprite-like mist slips in and out of sight, and there at the base of the range is the little store — a low white-washed shanty of one room; further up the slope in the clearing a gray log-cabin stands where Skimpy Sawyer lives.

Skimpy's father kept the store, in a leisurely and unexcited fashion — indeed many people might have considered that the store kept itself. As Ike dismounted and hitched the mare to the fence, he gave a peculiar whistle, a preconcerted signal, loud and shrill enough to summon his friend if he had been anywhere in the vicinity. No one responded, and Ike took his way to the open door of the store.

He had a certain pleasant anticipation; here congregated the mountain cronies, and he loved to listen to their talk enriched with warlike reminiscences, through which vibrated, as it were, some faint and far-off echo of the strain of the bugle and the roll of the drum.

His hopes were suddenly destroyed. As he ascended the three or four unhewn rocks that formed the steps to the door, he heard the long, expressionless drawl of the storekeeper within, and then a fat man's husky laugh. Ike started guiltily at the sound. But the broad sunshine had thrown a squatty shadow of him upon the floor within, and he knew that this caricature was recognized, for the voice sang out suddenly — "Ai — yi Ike; I see ye! Need n't be hidin'! I'll kem arter ye!"

Then as the boy, shamefaced and a little lowering, appeared in the doorway, he continued, "Whar's that buckeye tree ye war a-goin' ter cut down fur me so brash?"

"I plumb furgot it," mumbled Ike, as if his contrition were more acceptable when half articulate. "I furgot it, Mr. Corbin."

"I'll be bound ye did!" said the fat man vivaciously.

He was seated in one of the rickety chairs which hardly seemed adequate to his weight. He wore an unbleached cotton shirt, a suit of blue jeans much creased and crumpled, and a broad-brimmed hat, beneath which was a face also creased and crumpled. He was slow and inactive rather than old, and a man of his age who had lived a different life would hardly have such gray hair as his, or so many wrinkles. Nevertheless he had not entirely subsided into the chimney corner as is the habit of the elderly mountaineer. He still plied his trade which was that of making spinning-wheels and chairs, bread troughs and bowls, which require mechanical dexterity rather than agility; thus it was that he had hired Ike to find and cut down a sound and stalwart buckeye suitable for his purposes, his own unwieldy bulk and sedentary habits making him averse to undertaking the job himself.

Peter Sawyer, the storekeeper, was tall and lank. He had a long head, an attenuated face, and a habit of basking in the sun, which was not incongruous with a certain lizard-like aspect. He sat now with his chair tilted against the frame of the doorway, and the sunshine poured through upon him. He too wore his hat, and did not move while one of his customers counted some pelts that he had brought to exchange and announced the result. "Want some sugar an' salt fur 'em?" demanded the merchant lazily. "He'p yerse'f, neighbor; he'p yerse'f."

The neighbor, who lived on the other side of the mountain, pottered around among the merchandise in search of the sugar and salt, attended only by the storekeeper's dog, an earnest-minded and grave-mannered brute, that guarded the store by night and seemed to clerk there by day, following the customers about with sedulous politeness, and apparently only hindered from waiting upon them by the lack of adaptability in his paws. His urbanity did not extend to their followers. He measured strength with all the dogs that came to the store. It was useless for any pacifically disposed hound to sit under the wagon bed at a safe distance. The clerk would rush out with a celerity that implied a hundred feet, and the fracas under the wagon would be long and loud and bloody. But he had not all the canine pluck in the Big Smoky, and thus it was that one of his ears was slit, and he preferred to shut one eye, and his tail was but a stump. He turned wagging it vivaciously as Ike came in, and the storekeeper, regardless of old Corbin's reproofs, said benignantly, "Howdy, Ike, howdy? Make yerse'f at home. How's the fambly, Ike, how's the fambly?"

"Jes' toler'ble," said Ike, taking a rickety chair near the door.

"Uncle Ab ez well ez common?" demanded the customer, still hunting about for the salt. He was a tall, straight, soldierly fellow, and though he had fought on the opposite side he felt a comrade-like sympathy for the blinded artillery-man.

"He be jes' ez peart ez ever — jes' a-settin'-back," said Ike, with responsive interest. He had great love for his uncle and a special veneration for a man so learned as he fancied Abner Guyther to be in the science of gunnery. "He air jes' ez lively ez a three-year-old colt."

"Ain't he a heap o' trouble ter lead about an' sech?" demanded old Corbin, turning his crow's-feet — one could hardly have said his glance, for it was so deeply enveloped among the folds of wrinkles — upon Ike.

"Naw sir!" the boy repudiated the idea with a glowing cheek and a flashing eye. "Uncle Ab air sech good comp'ny everybody in the fambly jes' hankers ter bide nigh him; the identical dogs fight one another fur which one air ter be 'lowed ter lead him — sometimes ef we-uns air busy he walks with a string ter the dog's neck. Shucks! the main thing air to *git* ter lead him — jes' ez apt ez not uncle Ab will set out by his lone self. An' he don't often run over ennything — he 'pears ter hev a heap o' sense in his hands, an' he knows whenst he air a-comin' towards ennything like a door or post, though he 'll walk ag'in cheers or tubs or sech. 'Tother day — ye mought hev knocked me down I war so surprised — I kem along the road 'bout a quarter 'o a mile from home, an' thar sot uncle Ab a-top o' the rail fence — jes' a-settin' thar in the sun all alone an' a-whistlin' the bugle calls."

"Ho! ho!" exclaimed the customer, "he always hed spunk, — Abner hed; an' he air a-showin' it now, jes' ez true ez when he sarved in his battery."

"Yes, sir!" exclaimed Ike, gratified by this sign of appreciation. Then warming to the subject he continued, "Uncle Ab ain't 'feared o' nuthin' — not even now, in the everlastin' dark ez he be. Why, 't other day I see a old cannon-ball a-layin' on a ledge over yander at Keedon Bluffs, an' when he learn 'bout'n it he war plumb trembly, he war so excited, an' he 'lowed he 'd go ef I 'd holp him a leetle, an' climb down them tremenjious cluffs, jes' ter lay his hand on that cannon-ball, ter remind hisself o' that thar old gun o' his 'n, what he doted on so. It fairly bruk his heart ter spike it. I hev heard him tell 'bout'n it a-many-a-time."

"Hey!" exclaimed Peter Sawyer, turning about in amaze, "a blind man climb down Keedon Bluffs! 'T would take a mighty spry feller with all his senses fur that. I misdoubts ef ennybody hev ever done sech ez that — thout 't war Ab whenst he war young an' limber, an' wild ez a buck."

Ike had become suddenly conscious that old Corbin was watching him curiously.

"He don't 'pear ter know he air blind, do he?" demanded the fat man, slowly.

Ike detected some covert meaning in the tones. " Waal," he said, vaguely embarrassed and swinging his foot against the rung of the chair, " Uncle Ab — he jes' sets an' laffs, an' talks 'bout whar he hev been an' what him an' his comrades done, an' he don't notice much what's goin' on now, nor look out fur nuthin' ez is ter kem."

" He ain't soured noways," put in the customer, still intent on his purchase.

There was a momentary silence. The flies buzzed about the sorghum barrel. You might have heard the cat purring on the shelf.

" This hyar 'bout fair medjure, Pete ? " the customer demanded lifting his grave eyes as he helped himself to salt.

" I reckon so; I reckon so," said the storekeeper casually.

Ike rose abruptly in awkward and eager haste ; in a constrained and nervous way he asked for the logwood he wanted. His quick instincts had detected fault in something that he had said or the meaning that he had conveyed. But his penetration was not so subtle as to descry wherein the fault consisted. He was eager to get away. "'Fore I let my jaw git ter wabblin' ag'in. An' then I hed better cut off the e-end o' my tongue with a hatchet an' mebbe it would n't be so powerful nimble."

He expected old Corbin to say more, but the fat man sat solemnly puffing his pipe, his face more than usually wrinkled, as he watched Ike with his small twinkling eyes while Peter Sawyer procured the logwood and gave it to the boy.

With some indefinite intention of propitiation Ike turned toward him at the door. "I hev been toler'ble busy lately, but I'm a-goin' ter cut down that thar tree this evening, sure."

"So do! So do!" assented old Corbin unreservedly. "Then I'll gin ye that thar rooster I war a-tellin' ye 'bout. Powerful spry Dominicky."

Ike looked back over his shoulder once as he trotted off on the old white mare. The storekeeper and his clerk were standing in the doorway; the ex-soldier had completed his purchases, and was riding off toward the mountain; old Corbin was visible sitting within the door, a hand on either knee, his eyes meditatively downcast. He solemnly shook his head as he cogitated, and Ike was moved to wonder what he meant by it. "I wisht I hed n't tole what uncle Ab say 'bout climbin' down them bluffs. They 'pear ter think it be so cur'ous."

And it was of Abner Guyther that the two gossips were talking as Ike rode away out of sight.

"That be a powerful strange thing fur Abner ter be a-sayin'," remarked the storekeeper presently.

Old Corbin shook his head with a wise look; a wise smile wrinkled about the corners of his mouth.

"In my opinion *he* ain't no blind man. He kin see *some*, mebbe more, mebbe less. He air jes' purtendin'. Set up thar an' laff an' joke ez spry ez a boy o' twenty, an' talk 'bout climbin' down the bluffs — an' tell me he ain't hed his vision for all these years! I know Abner!"

"What makes ye 'low sech ez that, Jake?"

demanded his crony, fairly startled out of his composure by this proposition.

"Kase Abner always war a 'sateful an' a plottin' boy — look at the way he fooled his folks when he run off ter jine the Secesh! I ain't furgittin' that. An sure 's ye air born thar 's suthin' behind all them thar shet eyeballs. Abner, he hain't quit his plannin' an' sech. He hev got his reason fur it. It 's slow a-showin'. But it 'll be made plain."

The storekeeper puffed his cob-pipe, and silently watched the blue wreaths curl from it. He did not enter readily into this opinion, for he was a man of the practical views natural to those who associate much with their fellows. Despite the sparse population of the district he had a pivotal participation in such life as there was on the slopes and in the cove, for it revolved about the store. But Corbin spent his days in mere mechanical labor that left his mind free to wander. Thus speculation and vague fancies were his companions, and there was scant wonder that he should presently treat them as conclusions and facts.

In silent anticipation of the elucidation of the singular theory advanced, Peter Sawyer drew from his pocket a strong clasp knife and began to whittle a bit of wood which he picked up from the doorstep. But old Corbin's next remark seemed to have no relation to the subject.

"Who d'ye reckon I seen yestiddy up yander by that thar big vine-grown spot what they calls Old Scratch's vineyard?"

Pete Sawyer looked inquiringly doubtful, but silently puffed his pipe.

"*Jerry Binwell!*"

Old Corbin paused after he said this, smiling broadly and fixedly — all the wrinkles about his mouth and eyes seemed to come out as if to enjoy the sensation that this announcement occasioned.

The storekeeper stared blankly for a moment, then dropped his pipe upon the ground. The fire rolled out.

"Laws-a-massy!" he exclaimed, unheeding.

"Yes, sir! same old Jerry; the wuss fur wear; some *de*-lapidated; but — same old Jerry!"

"I 'lowed he war in Texas; folks said he went thar arter the war."

"I hailed him; he purtended not ter know me a-fust, an' he stopped, an' we talked awhile. He 'lowed he had never been ter Texas. Jes' down the kentry a piece in Persimmon Cove. I dunno whether he war tellin' the truth."

"I reckon he war," said the storekeeper. "It air a mighty out-o'-the-way place — Persimmon Cove; Satan hisself mought hid out in Persimmon an' folks in gineral never be the wiser ez the Enemy war enny nigher."

"He 'lowed he married thar," continued Corbin. "An' what d'ye reckon he hed along o' him?"

He looked at his crony with a broad grin.

"A — leetle gal! Thar they war a-travelin' along the slope. Hed a leetle ox-cart an' a steer geared up in it; he hed a cow critter too; calf followed; an' sech cheers an' housestuff ez he owned piled in the cart, an' settin' a-top o' it all this hyar leetle gal — 'bout ez big ez a shingle. She rid, bein' ez she hain't got no weight sca'cely."

"An' whar's the 'oman?" asked the storekeeper, missing an important factor in the family circle.

Corbin lowered his voice and his humorous wrinkles strove to retire themselves.

"Dead," he said gravely.

Peter Sawyer, bethinking himself of his pipe, filled it anew with a crumpled leaf of tobacco, relighted it, and with the pipe-stem between his teeth resumed the conversation.

"An' what sorter welcome do he reckon he air goin' ter find 'mongst the mountings hyar. Do he 'low we hev furgot his sheer in the war, kase it hev been right smart time since? Naw sir. I 'members like yestiddy whenst old Jeemes Guyther — Abner's dad, ye know — kem ter my store, lookin' ez ef he hed buried all his kin on yearth, an' tole ez Abner hed run off ter jine the Secesh along o' Jerry Binwell. An' the old man said he hoped Ab mought die afore he reached the Rebel lines, kase he 'd ruther mourn him dead 'n know he hed raised his hand ag'in the Nunion."

"But he would n't, though," said Corbin prosaically. "Them war days when men talked mighty big."

"An' they acted mighty big too, sometimes," retorted Sawyer.

"Waal, Abner war the apple o' the old man's eye," said Corbin; "I b'lieve he'd turn in his grave ef he could know how Ab war hurt. The whole fambly jes' the same, too. Look how Ab air pompered now. Ef Abner war blind sure enough he could n't be better treated. His dad always put the blame o' Ab's goin' on Jerry. An' Jerry war a wuthless chance! He kem back inside o' a year — deserted! But Ab never kem back till arter the s'render."

"What makes ye 'low ez Abner hev got his vision same ez common?" Sawyer demanded again. "That notion 'pears powerful cur'ous ter me — seein' him led about hyar fur nigh on ter twenty year, now by Ike, an' now by his brother, an' then ag'in by a dog an' sech."

Old Corbin looked cautiously over his shoulder through the open door as if he feared some lurking eaves-dropper. The cabin on the slope stood silent and motionless in the motionless yellow radiance of the autumnal sun. But the winds were astir, and as they swayed the woods they revealed bizarre sunbeams rioting hither and thither in glittering fantasies among the leaves. No one sauntered down the curves of the winding road nor along the banks of the shining river. The only creature visible was the old dog asleep, but sitting upright, in a dislocated posture, his head nodding spasmodically, and his lower jaw dropped.

"Ye hearn," said Corbin softly, "that thar nevy o' his, Ike Guyther, 'low Ab want ter climb down Keedon Bluffs ter whar that old ball's a-lyin'. Now do ye reckon a *blind* man ez hev got good sense air goin' ter trest his bones a-gittin' down that jagged bluff ez sheer ez a wall with sech holp ez that thar skitter-brained Ike kin gin?"

Sawyer, holding his pipe in one hand and his grizzled chin in the other, meditatively shook his head.

"Naw sir," said Corbin, putting the gesture into the more stalwart negation of words. "A man, though, ez hed his vision, though his j'ints be stiff some with age and laziness, mought do it, special ef he hed the holp o' some strong spry boy like Ike, cz be astonishin' grown fur his age, but ain't got no mo' sense an' scrimination than a boy naterally hev."

Once more Peter Sawyer nodded his head — this time the action was vertical, for the gesture intimated affirmation.

"What in the name o' reason do Abner want ter go down whar the old ball be lodged?" he asked in a speculative voice, as if he hardly expected an answer.

But the ready Corbin, primed with surmises, first looked cautiously up and down the road and then ventured a suggestion.

"Waal, sir; seein' Jerry Binwell minded me o' Abner Guyther, an' how they used ter consort together, an' thinkin' o' Ab 'minded me o' the store old Squair Torbett used ter set on him. Ab war mighty nigh always at the Squair's house a-doin' some leetle job or other, special arter the Squair tuk ter agein' so through worryin' 'bout the war an' his sons ez war in the army. An' Jerry Binwell war at the Squair's too, bein' Ab's shadder. Waal, ye know the Squair hed a power o' money, an' he hed drawed it out'n the banks in the valley towns, 'count o' the raidin' soldiers an' sech. An' he hid it somehows. Some 'lowed he buried it, but most folks said he let these hyar two boys inter the secret, an' Ab clomb down an' hid the money in a strong box in a hole in Keedon Bluffs, whilst Jerry watched. Ye hev hearn that word? Waal, sir, the Bluffs air like a honeycomb; so full o' holes ef a body did n't know which one they hid it in they could n't find it."

"I hev hearn folks a-talkin' 'bout it myself," put in Pete Sawyer, "though o' late years they hev gin that up, mos'ly."

"Yessir," assented Corbin. "An' the g'rillas they s'arched the Squair's house ag'in an' ag'in, an' could n't find nuthin'. These two boys hed run off ter the Secesh army, by that time, else they 'd hev been made ter tell whar the plunder war hid. An' though Jerry deserted an' kem back, the Southern sympathizers would n't let him bide one single night in the cove, but druv him off, an' he ain't dared ter show his face hyar sence, else I reckon he 'd hev stole the money, ef he hed knowed whar it war — the Squair being dead mighty onexpected."

The storekeeper's eyes widened. "Ye — 'low — the — money 's — thar — yit — hid in Keedon Bluffs?" he panted.

"I know this," said old Corbin. "'T war hid thar, an' I hearn with my own ears the heirs say they never got no money out 'n Keedon Bluffs — they fairly scouted the idee. An' now," he pursued, "one of the heirs is dead; an' the t' other 's moved ter Arkansas. An' hyar kems one o' the men ez watched whilst the money war hid; an' the t' other ez hid it — a *blind* man — be in a mighty hurry an' disturbament ter climb down Keedon Bluffs. I dunno why they hain't got it afore. I can't foller percisely the serpient trail of the evil men. But ye mark my words — them two fellers will hev a powerful big row — or" — his eyes twinkled — "they 'll divide the plunder an' ye 'll hear o' them consortin' tergether like frien's."

He met with a triumphant leer the distended astonished gaze of the storekeeper.

"Ho! ho! Keedon Bluffs don't speak 'less

they be spoke to fust," he continued, "but thar secrets git noised abroad. Thar's suthin' thar wuth layin' hands on 'thout foolin' along of a old spent cannon-ball."

V.

THE arrival of Jerry Binwell and his little girl at Hiram Guyther's cabin soon became known throughout the Cove, and the fact, which Ike shortly discovered, that the newcomers were regarded with disfavor by others did not tend to further commend them to him. He felt an odd sinking of the heart and a grotesque sort of mortification whenever he went to the mill or the store and encountered questions and comments concerning his father's guests. Sometimes he was taken aside by a conservative old codger, and the queries were propounded in a mysterious and husky whisper which imparted additional urgency.

"They tell me ez *Jerry Binwell* air a-visitin' yer dad — air that a true word?"

And Ike would sulkily nod.

"What did he kem fur?"

"Ter get out 'n the storm."

"Storm 's been over a week an' better" —

with an implacable logic. Then, dredging with new energy for information — "When's he goin' away?"

"Dunno."

"Whar's he goin' ter?" persistently.

"Dunno."

"What's he doin' of?" changing the base of attack.

"Nuthin'."

"What's he say?"

"Ennything."

"Waal sir!" in a tone of disappointment, the whole examination resulting in the total amount of nothing.

Out of Ike's presence public opinion expressed itself more freely and it was unanimous. No one denied that it was a strange thing that Hiram Guyther, one of the most solid, respectable, and reliable men of the whole country-side, whose very name was a guarantee of good faith, should be harboring a graceless, worthless, neer-do-weel like Jerry Binwell, who was, moreover, suspected of treachery which had resulted in Abner's blindness. The lines of demarkation between those of high character and those who lack the sterling virtues are strongly drawn and rigorously observed in the mountains. The stern and grim old Hiram himself was forced to recognize the incongruity of the situation and its utter irreconcilability with the popular estimation of himself and his household. But he maintained his ground as well as he might.

"Yaas," he would drawl, "Jerry's a-puttin' up with we-uns now. Dunno how long he'll stay. Till the spring o' the year, mebbe. Naw, him an' Abner don't clash none. Naw, he don't pester me, nuther."

And with these baffling evasions he would ride away, leaving the gossips at the store or the mill drawing their chairs closer together, and knitting their brows, and shaking their heads.

It was all most ominous and depressing to Ike, for he was proud and keenly sensitive to any decline in public esteem; sometimes he was fairly tempted to tell that the old folks at his house had fallen victims to the witching charms of a noisy little body three feet high, who made them like everything she did, and do things of which they would never have believed themselves capable. Thus they tolerated Jerry for her sake. And then he held his peace for fear the gossips would say they were all touched in the head.

For certain severe elderly people who had visited the house — it had more visitors than usual — had observed in his hearing that they were sorry for his mother and his aunt Jemima ; — " ter be cluttered up at thar time o' life with a young child, special sech a one ez that, ez could no mo' stan' still 'n a pea on a hot shovel, an' war a-laffin' an' a-hollerin' all the time till a-body couldn't hear thar own ears."

Ike felt peculiar resentment against the propounders of these strictures, although he had not consciously fallen under the fascination of the little Rosamond. He could not however always disregard her hilarious challenges to play, but when he succumbed it was with a sort of surly surprise at his own relenting. He even consented to see-saw with her, — a pastime which she greatly affected, — although he was obliged to sit on a very short end of the plank thrust between the rails of the fence in order to balance her very small weight as she sat at the other extremity, on the inside of the fence. And there, as she swayed high and dropped low, beaming with smiles and pink with delight, she looked like a veritable rose, blown about in the playful wind. But Ike was less picturesque as he bobbed up and down very close indeed to the rails and the leaning cross-stakes. "I'll butt my brains out ag'in these rails like a demented Billy-goat if I don't mind," he said to himself in dudgeon.

One day, when he and Skimpy had been visiting certain traps that they had jointly set in the woods, their homeward way led them past the store. They had had good luck with their snares, and their fine spirits responded alertly to a robust chorusing laugh that suddenly rang out from the dark interior of the building.

The boys quickened their steps; there was something unusual going on inside.

The brown, unpainted walls within, the shadowy beams and dusky rafters above, the burly boxes and barrels in the background, were dimly illumined by the one fibrous slant of sunshine through the window, which served to show too the long gaunt figure of the storekeeper standing near the entrance. He was swaying backward, laughing as he smote his thigh, and he called out, "Do it ag'in, Shanks! Do it ag'in!"

Then the boys observed that there was a large group of figures standing at one side, although not easily distinguishable since their brown jeans garb so assimilated with the mellow tint of the walls. The next minute Ike reached the door and the whole scene was distinct before him. In the midst of the circle stood Jerry Binwell, his coat lying on the floor, his hat hanging on the knob of a rickety chair. His thin, long face was flushed; he was laughing too and rubbing his hands, and walking to and fro a few steps each way. "Do it ag'in, Shanks," once more called out Peter Sawyer.

There were friendly enough glances bent upon him, and everybody was laughing pleasantly, despite the pipes held between strong discolored teeth. Even old Jake Corbin had a reluctant twinkle among the many wrinkles that encircled his eyes as he sat smoking, his rickety chair tilted back against the wall.

"Pritty spry yit, fur a ole man," declared Binwell, still rubbing his hands.

"Do it ag'in, Shanks!" rang out from the bystanders.

Binwell looked up for a moment, drawing back to the extreme end of the apartment. Suddenly he crouched and sprang into the air with an incredible lightness. It was a long oblique jump to the beam on which he caught; he did not wait a second but "skinned the cat" among the rafters with an admirable dexterity and dropped softly on his feet at the doorway.

Once more there was a guffaw. "Go it, Shanks!" "He's a servigrous jumper, sure!" "Spry as a deer!"

It was a most pacific scene and the exhibition of agility seemed likely to promote only good fellowship and the pleasant passing of the hour until old Corbin remarked:

"Yes, Jerry's a good jumper, an' a good runner, too, I hev hearn."

Binwell cast a quick glance over his shoulder; a light gleamed in his small, dark, defiant eye. Whether he did not pique himself on his speed, or whether he detected a sub-current of meaning in the comment, he was moved to demand abruptly:

"Whar did ye ever see me run?"

Old Corbin's delight in the opportunity broadened his face by an inch or two. The display of intricate hieroglyphic wrinkles about his eyes was more than one might imagine possible to be described by age and fatness. His mouth distended to show the few teeth that had not yet forsaken his gums; his burly sides were shaking with laughter before he said, "I never *seen* ye run, Jerry, but I hearn ez ye done some mighty tall runnin' in the old war time."

There was a shout of derision from the crowd, most of the men having served in one army or the other. The object of this barbed ridicule looked as if he might sink through the floor. His face flushed, his abashed eyes dropped, he stood quivering and abject before them all.

Ike had a quick pang of pity and resentment. And yet he was ashamed that this was the man who sat by his father's hearth and shared their bread.

It was only for a moment that he was sorry for Binwell. The recovery from all semblance of shame or wounded pride was instantaneous as he retorted:

"That's mighty easy ter say 'bout ennybody." He whirled around on his light heel. "Naw, folks," he cried out, "I ain't much on the run; never footed it more 'n jes' fairly. But I tell ye — ef ye be tired o' seein' me jump — my jumpin' ain't nuthin' ter my heftin'. I kin lift the heaviest man hyar an' jump with him. Less see," he affected to turn about and survey the burly, stalwart crowd. "Who pulls the beam at the highest figger?"

He hesitated for a moment; then with a sudden dart that was like the movement of a fish, he seized on old Corbin.

"Naw! naw!" wheezed the fat old fellow as the stringy, muscular arms encircled him. He strove to hold to his chair; it fell over in the fracas and eluded his grasp; he clutched at the window-sill — vainly; his hat dropped off; his face was scarlet, and he roared for help.

It would doubtless have been extended had not the quick and agile Jerry forestalled the heavy mountaineers. He lifted Corbin with a mighty effort; he even carried out his boast of jumping — not high, after all, but high enough for the wildly clutching old man to catch the low beam with both hands.

Binwell suddenly loosed his hold and left him swaying ponderously to and fro, two or three feet from the floor, in imminent danger of falling, sputtering and wheezing, and red in the face and with eyes starting out of his head. Then his tormentor, fearful doubtless of the recoil of public opinion, caught up his hat and coat and with a loud scornful laugh ran out of the store and disappeared up the leafy road.

To a man of ordinary weight and agility it would have been easy enough to spring to the floor. But the cumbersome bulk and slow, clumsy habit of old Corbin lent the situation real danger. There was a rush to his assistance — some officious hand thrust an empty barrel beneath his feet, hoping to afford him support, but it toppled under his weight and down he came, amidst a great rending of staves, as the barrel collapsed beneath him.

He was unhurt, although greatly shaken. He had been frightened at first; perhaps there was never so angry a man in the limits of the Cove as he was now. Again and again, as he was helped to his chair, he declared that he would revenge himself on Jerry Binwell, and the sympathetic crowd expressed their sense of the injury and the danger to which he had been subjected, as well as the indignity offered him. To Ike's extreme amazement Binwell's name was often coupled with that of his father, or the blind man, his uncle. Now, ordinarily, Ike would have felt that these two spirited and responsible people were amply able to answer for themselves; but he knew that it was only by an odd combination of circumstances that they were associated, almost with the intimacy of family relations, with such a person as Binwell. It implied a friendship for him which he knew they did not feel, and an indorsement of him which they were not prepared to give. Secure in their own sense of rectitude and good repute this possibility of a decline in public esteem had never, he was sure, occurred to them. Alas, Rosamondy, he heartily regretted that she had ever put her dimpled foot across their threshold, and yet he stipulated again within himself that it was not in his heart to wish any houseless creatures out of the shelter they had found.

He had a vague terror of this false position in which the family was placed. He knew, with suddenly awakened forecast, that the antagonism to Jerry Binwell would not end here. Old Corbin's spleen that might once have passed for naught was now rendered a valid and righteous anger in public opinion, and he would have the sympathy and aid of all the country-side. But how or why, in the name of justice, could it include his father and his blind uncle, who had done naught after all but feed the hungry, and forgive the enemy, and house the roofless vagrant.

He lingered for a time after old Corbin had gone to Sawyer's house to get "a bite an' rest his bones," listening to the younger men discuss the incident, and comment on Binwell's strength.

When Ike at last rose and started, Skimpy started too.

"Skimp!" called the storekeeper after him, "yer mam's got suthin' fur ye to do at the house. Go thar!"

Skimpy obediently turned from the road into the by-path and Ike went on, his heart swelling with indignation and his eyes hot with tears. He knew that his friend was to be withheld from his association after this, lest he might come under the influence of so worthless and injurious an example as Jerry Binwell. He trudged along home, wishing that his father might have beheld the scene and wondering if that would have urged him to take some decided action in the case.

Ike had an odd indisposition to relate it all. He had been trained in a maxim, — good enough so far as it goes, — "If you can't say anything kind of your neighbor, say nothing." The only manifestation of his opinion was expressed in deeds, not in words. His mother had looked sharply at him from time to time during the past week, and this afternoon, as she opened suddenly the shed-room door and saw him casting down a great pile of bark, and chips, and sticks of wood, ready for the morning fires, she said unexpectedly:

"Ike, ain't ye ailin' nowhar?"

"Naw 'm," he replied, drawing himself up with stalwart pride, "I feel ez solid an' sound ez a rock."

"I 'lowed ye mus' be sick — ye 'pear so sober-faced, an' occupy yerself no ways sca'cely, 'cept in workin' — tendin' on the wood-pile, an' packin' the water, an' drivin' the cow-critter. I ain't hed ez much wood hyar ter burn, nor water ter cook with, nor the cow ez constant at the bars, fur ten year."

Ike turned and glanced reflectively about him. The mountain, gorgeous in autumnal array, loomed above; a blue sky looked pensively down; some aerial craft had spread a cloud-sail, and the wind was fair.

"I never 'lowed ter feel sech pleasure in a

wood-pile," he said, meditatively. "I hev made up my mind ez I ain't a-goin' ter ondertake to be a shirk in this world."

She understood him instantly. As the door swung a little ajar she looked back over her shoulder through the shed-room into the main room of the cabin. Binwell was not there; no one was visible in the ruddy glare of the fire illuminating the brown walls but the little Rosamond and the blind man. She had elected to consider herself some neighing, prancing steed, and Abner held her by one long, golden curl, that served as reins. A short tether, to be sure, but she curveted, and stamped, and laughed as few horses have ever done. The reflection of her merriment was in the smile on the blind man's face. Her very shadow was glad, as it sported with the firelight on the floor.

VI.

THERE is nothing so conducive to happiness as work — work done well and willingly. It is in itself happiness. Ike wondered to find, as he bent his mind and all his energy to his simple tasks — grown strangely light and seeming few — how little he suffered from his exclusion from his friend's society and from the unjust discrimination made against him for no fault of his; how amply his duty filled his horizon, and presently arrayed itself in the glad garb of pleasure. He sang — he could but sing — as he wielded the axe, as he fed the stock, as he went back and forth on his errands through the lonely woods, sometimes hearing the voice of Keedon Bluffs singing too, in fitful and fugue-like response.

Nevertheless, he was glad enough to be reassured of his friend's loyalty in their enforced separation, for when they presently met by accident Skimpy seized upon him eagerly,

"Ye ain't holdin' no gredge ag'in *me*, air ye, Ike? I couldn't holp it; ye know I couldn't."

This accidental meeting occurred one evening when all the boys of Tanglefoot Cove and the mountain slopes had gathered for a coon-hunt. The Sawyer lads were of the party, Skimpy and three brothers, all much alike, all long-legged, red-haired, freckled-faced fellows, and not fascinating to look upon, but they took a great deal of pleasure in themselves, and there was considerable boy-nature to the square inch in these four Sawyers. They were first-rate comrades too; could both take a joke and make one; all had bright, honest, steady brown eyes, and they were evidently destined to grow better looking as they grew older. With one exception they were clad in whole, stout homespun garments, well woven and well made, for their mother was a peculiarly precise, neat, and industrious woman. Skimpy was the exception; his elbows were out; his ankles could not wait for his trousers to grow, so they showed themselves, right nimble and sturdy members, although the garment, which was blue, had been encouraged lengthwise with a fresh contrasting piece of copper-colored jeans; his knees bulged against the threadbare cloth in a way that intimated they would not long be able to shelter themselves in their flimsy retirement. He and his mother found it difficult to reconcile their diverse theories of the uses and the care of clothes. Although serious enough when they climaxed, these differences had no depressing effect on Skimpy's spirits, and did not suffice to save his wardrobe. He harbored no unfilial resentment, but he thought his mother a very queer and particular woman.

The Sawyers had brought with them the dutiful clerk, who was also preëminent as a coon-dog. There he sat in his yellow hide, decorated with his slit ear, and his docked tail, and his half-closed eyelid. When away from the store his demeanor lacked the urbanity which characterized him there. He bore himself now with the surly air of a magnate whose affability has been swallowed up in the consciousness of importance.

The Sawyers specially piqued themselves on being the proud possessors of Bose. Every now and then one would reverently glance at the animal, as he sat upright lolling out an indifferent tongue, and say to those unacquainted with him — "Mind how ye fool with Bose — he's sharp" (with an excited eye and a wag of the red head); "he's mighty fierce." And the other Sawyers would nod their heads in confirmation of this report of Bose's belligerent qualities. They had a sort of hero-worshiping reverence for this trait of dog-sharpness, but any one who did not think respectfully of Bose was some one who did not care to go coon-hunting. He was the central figure of the group that had collected in the woods by a sulphur spring, on a slope of one of the minor ridges at the base of the Great Smoky. The early dusk had not yet fallen, but the shadows were lengthening fast, and night was on the way. The boughs of the trees above their heads were drawn in fine distorted lines on a crimson sky; here and there a slant of sunshine fell amongst the brown shadows upon some red and yellow fantasy of foliage that so blazed with color and light in its dusky surroundings that it might seem some outburst of fire which had been slyly " set out " in the woods.

The sulphur spring had sought to hide itself, it might seem. Across a narrow, rocky cleft lay a great flat slab, and a rill trickled away somewhere; no one would have imagined that beneath this slab was a spring with brown crystalline water, and a vibrant whisper, and some exquisite perfumed breath of freshness borrowed from the dawn of day. The dogs knew where it was, running to it with lolling tongues and with much affectation of thirst, yet wanting only a drop or two. For other dogs were there and they seemed to have heard and to have profited by the Sawyers' account of Bose, or perhaps the dignity of his mien awed them, or experience admonished them, for none of them molested him, although they became involved in noisy fights with each other, or gambols as turbulent. The boys, ten or twelve in number, all had cow-horns to blow and torches to carry, and while they waited for certain cronies to arrive the talk was chiefly of the subject that had brought them together. The coon seemed a fascinating study apart from his great gifts of celerity. Mentally he is generously endowed. If Skimpy might be believed the coon can do anything short of reading, writing, and ciphering.

"Even mam, she hev ter 'low ez coons ain't lackin' fur head-stuffin'," he remarked, as he stood with his arms akimbo. "You-uns know the kind o' ways mam hev gin herself over ter — a-sweepin', an' a-scourin', an' a-cleanin', till I actially looks ter see ef she won't take ter washin' the chickens' faces an' curryin' the cat. Waal, Cousin Eph Bates, he stopped thar one day with his pet coon. An' mam she made him welcome an' set out the table. An' mam, she 'lowed the coon mus' be hongry, so she called it an' gin it a nice piece o' corn dodger. What's that coon do?" he cried, his eyes widening with the interest of the recital. "Popped up on the aidge o' the drinkin' pail an' ondertook ter wash that thar piece o' dodger 'twixt his fore paws, 'fore he would eat it. I wish ye could hev seen mam's face. I laffed till I like ter drapped in my tracks. An' Cousin Eph — he jes' hollered. An' mam, she hed furgot, ef she ever knowed, how coons do; she say, 'Cousin Eph, ye need n't bring no sech pertic'lar vis'tor ter my house ag'in — a-washin' the clean vittles *I* gin him.' Thar sot the coon, ez onconsarned, a-washin' his hands an' a-washin' the dodger." Skimpy suited the action to the words and teetered up and down, washing his paws and an imaginary piece of corn dodger. "I laffed an' laffed. That coon like ter been the death o' me 'fore he got away from thar."

"I know that thar coon o' Eph Bates's," cried Ike. "I stayed up ter his house one night along o' his chill'n an' 'twar bright moonlight whenst I went ter bed in the roof-room, but after a while I woke up an' I 'lowed 'twar a hailstorm goin' on outside on the roof. Ye never hearn sech a skedaddlin' up an' down them clapboards. Kem ter find out, 'twar nuthin' but the coon a-playin' tag with his shadder in the moonlight."

"Oh, he's powerful tricky, Mister Coon air," Skimpy declared, his freckled face distended with relish of Mr. Coon's smartness. "Mam an' Cousin Eph hed sot tharselfs down afore the fire an' got ter talkin' 'bout'n the folkses in the Cove, an' how mighty few o' 'em had enny sech religion ez they purtended ter hev, when mam she put her hand in her pocket fur ter git her knittin'. An' there warn't nuthin' in her pocket but a ball o' yarn. An' she looked up, an' thar war a great long e-end o' it a-stretchin' ter the door. An' thar on the steps sot Mister Coon with them knittin' needles, an' the sock, a-holdin' 'em like he war knittin', ez onconsarned — oh my! I laffed ag'in."

"I'll bet yer mam did n't laff," said an intimate of the family.

"Naw," Skimpy admitted. "Mam, she's mighty sober-sided. She'd like the coon better ef he wore spec's an' cut wood. Cousin Eph, he axed her how many rows that coon knit. An' mam, she said — '*None!* He drug two needles bodaciously out an' spiled fower rows.' Mam 'lowed ez she thought she hed the mos' mischievious created critter — meanin' me — but she said she b'lieved Cousin Eph mought take the prem*ium*. An' Cousin Eph, he said enny time she war minded ter swap he'd trade the coon fur me. An' mam, she cut her eye round at me an' tole me I hed better mend my manners; the mounting would talk mightily 'bout me ef I war traded off fur a coon 'thout enny boot."

"That thar mus' be the same coon ez Cousin Eph Bates fotched along o' him ter the store when he kem ter trade, las' summer," said Obadiah, the eldest Sawyer. "An' dad, he tole Cousin Eph ter holp hisself. An' nobody noticed the coon till Cousin Eph war ready ter go, an' tuk ter huntin' fur him. I don't reckon that coon could surely hev thunk ez dad meant it fur *him* whenst he told Cousin Eph ter holp hisself. But leastwise the coon done it; he holped *his*-self. They fund him propped up on the aidge o' the sugar bar'l, an' they say the way his whiskers war gormed with sugar war a sight ter be seen. He hed n't no expression ter his face, an' he looked plumb cross-eyed with pleasure. Sugar in his paws, too, and dad kerried on like he war mighty nigh demented. An' he wanted Cousin Eph ter pay for that sugar the coon hed eat, an' said he wanted that thar coon's skin. But Cousin Eph, he snatched his coon up under his arm an' 'lowed he mought ez well try ter trade fur one o' his chill'n's hides. I b'lieve he gin dad some money or 'suthin', though. He sot out arter that with his coon fur home."

"Waal, he war n't so 'fectionate with that thar coon las' time I seen him," Ike added his testimony. "'Twar over yander at the church-house in the gap. An' whilst the folks war settin' inside, a-listenin' ter the preachin', we-uns hearn the biggest rumpus outside 'mongst the teams, an' everybody looked plumb wretched, wonderin' ef 'twar suthin' hed happened ter thar steer or horse critter. An' dad whispered ter me ter go out an' see. An' thar, 'mongst all the wagins, an' yokes o' oxen, an' saddle horses under the trees, war a young claybank horse ez b'long ter Eph Bates. An' that thar coon he had slyed off an' follered his master ter the church-house, an' stiddier goin' inside — it's a mercy he didn't — he seen Eph's horse, an' he clomb the tree, an' drapped down on the pommel o' the saddle. Waal, sir, sech kickin'! that horse war young an' skeery; sech squealin'! An' whenst I seen him he war tremblin' like he hed a fit o' the ague, an' then he'd turn his head an' git a glimge o' that thar citizen in the saddle, an' begin ter plunge an' shy an' snort ag'in. Jes' 'fore I got ter him he bruk his halter, an' he lit out; around an' around that thar church-house he went a-cavortin' an' a-gallopin', Mister Coon settin' in the saddle, a-holdin' on fur life, an' a-smilin' from ear to ear. An' the folks in the church-house seen what war a-goin' on, an' Eph an' some o' them nigh the door run out an' hollered, 'Whoa! Whoa!' at the horse. Didn't do no good. Ez soon ez the critter seen he couldn't shake the coon off he bolted an' run through the woods. Eph, he walked home that Sunday, five mile, but Mister Coon, he rid."

"Oh, Mister Coon, oh, Mister Coon," Skimpy was murmuring, and presently he broke into song: —

"Bob Snooks, he eat up all in his plate,
An' he dreampt a dream that night right late.
A-settin' on a cloud war a big raccoon,
A-eatin' an' a-washin' his paws in the moon.
'Twar brimmin' full o' clabber an' whey.
His tail war ringed with black an' gray;
It hung plumb down ter the poplar-tree,
An' he wagged it up an' down in glee.

CHORUS.

"Oh, Mister Coon! oh, Mister Coon,
Oh, take them dirty paws out 'n the moon.

"He looked at Bob, ter wink an' grin,
An' then Bob say — 'Ez sure ez sin
I'll yank ye off 'n the aidge o' that moon,
Though ye air a mos' surprisin' coon.'
Bob sicked on Towse — *Towse clomb the tree!*
An' grabbed the coon right nat'rally.
An' suddint Bob woke — thar war *no* raccoon,
Bob wisht he hed lef' him up thar on the moon.

CHORUS.

"Oh, Mister Coon! oh, Mister Coon,
Oh, why can't ye once more balance on the moon."

It was quite dark before they were fairly started. The shadows gloomed thick about them. The stars were in the sky. The sound of the boyish voices whooping and calling, and singing snatches of the coon-song, echoed far and wide among the solemn woods and the listening rocks. The dogs answered to the eager urgency of their masters by wheezing and snuffing about the ground as they ran with their muzzles down, but the best among them, even the preëminent Bose, could conjure no coon where no coon was.

"What ails 'em ter take ter sech a piece o' briars," Skimpy cried out suddenly with an accompaniment of a ripping sound. "Ef I tear up these hyar clothes o' mine enny mo' I'll hev some rents ter mend in my skin, fur my mother hev sot it down ef I gin her so many repairs ter make she'll gin me some."

This terrifying prospect did not unduly alarm Skimpy nor hinder his joyous pursuit of the coon. He was the first fellow to fall into the briars and to flounder into the branch. His nimble feet followed more closely than any others their canine precursors. It was he who cried out and encouraged the dogs and kept them together, and even the self-sufficient and experienced Bose hearkened to his counsel and lent himself to guidance. Skimpy was close upon the docked tail of this animal when suddenly the wheezing Bose emitted a short sharp cry and sprang off in the darkness with all the dogs after him.

VII.

THE moon was just beginning to rise. A vague red glow suffused the summit of the eastern mountains. It hardly revealed, but in some sort it suggested, the presence of the vast forests of the Cove, that still stood dusky and gloomily mysterious. The solemn silence, native to the solitudes, was for the nonce annihilated. The whole night seemed to ring with the shouting triumph of the boys. The cry of the dogs was unintermittent. Naught impeded the wild chase, save that now and then a projecting root caught an unwary foot, and a boy would go crashing to the ground, his companions jumping over his prostrate form, or perhaps falling upon him, then scrambling up together and away again hilariously. Sometimes a horn would sound, and if one had cared to listen he might have wondered to hear the countless blasts that the echoes wound, or laughed to fancy how that mimic chase in the air did fare. Sometimes, too, a voice would call out from the van of the line, "Oh, Mister Coon!" And anon Keedon Bluffs repeated the words in a solemn staccato, as if they were some uncomprehended incantation. "Oh, Mister Coon!"

What that gentleman thought of it all nobody can say. Whether he resented the fact that his coat was considered too good for him, and just good enough for a cap for somebody else; or whether he felt complimented that he was esteemed so game that it was accounted a pleasure to see him fight, singly, a score of savage dogs, and die in the jaws of the enemies he crippled, nobody will ever know. The only certain thing is that he carried his fat and his fur, and his palpitating identity inside of them, as fast and as far as he could. And then in desperation he swiftly climbed a tree, and sat there panting, looking down with eyes whose dilated pupils defied the night, to mark how the fierce rout came at full cry over the rise. The boys knew what he had done, notwithstanding the dark forests that intervened, for the dogs announced in loud and joyful barks that the coon was treed as they besieged the oak, springing as high as they could about its trunk. There was a chorus, "Oh, Mister Coon!" from the hunters as they came pelting over the hill, almost dead beat with the run. For the coon had footed it bravely, and treeing him was long delayed.

The torches, skimming swiftly about under the oak, which was close upon a precipice, flared in the darkness far along the slopes, and the coon hunt glimpsed from the distant cove was like an errant constellation, run away from the skies. Nearer, flame and smoke flaunted back in the wind, showing the colors of a limited section of the autumn woods close about, and thus conjuring an oasis of gorgeous brilliance in that desert of gloom. In the radiance of the fringed flaring lights might be distinguished, in high relief against the dusky background, Ike's eager face, and Skimpy's hatchet-like features,— as he bent to beseech Bose to calm himself instead of bounding futilely about the tree which he could not climb like the dream-dog, — and the muscular poses of Obadiah Sawyer, who wielded the axe about the trunk of the tree. How the echoes answered! How the rocks rang with the stalwart strokes! The chips flew with every cleavage. The dogs leaped, and barked on every shrill key of impatience. The coon, barely visible, crouched in the darkness, growled, and looked down on his boisterous enemies. "Keep out 'n the way o' this axe, I tell ye," Obadiah Sawyer would cry as the backward motion would threaten one of the boys or their four-footed comrades, who pressed so close about the tree as to lose all sense of safety.

Suddenly, without any warning, the trunk of the tree not half severed, the coon ran down almost over Obadiah into the midst of the dogs. There was a frantic plunge amongst them; a fierce growling and yelping and snapping; a crunching of teeth; and now and then as one suffered the sharp fangs of the coon, a hideous clamor that seemed to pierce the sky.

The boys stood amazed at this innovation on the part of Mr. Coon, whose sense of etiquette does not usually permit him to tackle the dogs until the falling of the tree throws the hapless creature into their jaws. How he distinguished the sound in all that shrill tumult Skimpy could never say; — a low growl, exceeding in ferocity aught he had ever before heard, caught his attention. He moved back a pace and held the torch aloft. There, upon the bole of the tree, slowly descending from limb to limb, with lissome noiseless tread, with great yellow eyes, illuminated by the flare, was a full-grown female panther, made bold enough to face the light by the imminence of the danger, for the cutting down of the tree meant certain dislodgment amongst the dogs and the boys. This was the denizen of the oak, the discovery of whom had made the coon prefer the dogs.

Skimpy needed but a single glance. He said afterward that it flashed upon him in a moment that the animal's young were perhaps in a crevice of the great wall of rock close at hand, and that for this reason she had not fled from the noise and the lights. Skimpy dashed his torch to the ground, and crying "Painter! Painter!" he set out at a pace which has seldom been excelled. All the torches were flared upward. The creature glared down at the boys and growled. There was not a gun in the party. Obadiah in a sort of mental aberration flung his axe into the tree; it almost grazed the animal's nose, then fell upon the back of a yelping dog.

Each boy seemed to announce his flight by taking up the panic-stricken cry of "Painter!" The dogs had discovered that more had been treed than the coon, which at last had been killed. They would not heed the whistlings and the callings of their masters, and as the boys ran a tremendous yelping and growling announced that the panther had sprung from the tree amidst the pack. Presently something, with its tail between its legs, shot by the hindmost boy, and another, and yet another. The dogs had felt the panther's teeth and claws and were leaving, but none of these fugitives was Bose.

"Oh," cried Skimpy, "le's go back — le's go back — Bose will be bodaciously eat up! Le's go back an' call Bose off!"

"Call the painter on, ye mean!" exclaimed Ike. "Ye can't do nuthin' ter hurt a painter 'thout ye hed a gun!"

"Oh Bose!" plained another of the Sawyers in a heart-wrung voice. "What'll mam do 'thout Bose! Sech a shepherd! Sech a dog ter take keer o' the baby, too! Sech a gyard dog!" For Bose's virtues were not all belligerent, but shone resplendent in times of peace. "Oh *Bose*," he shrieked down the wind, "let the painter be!"

"Oh *Bose!*" cried Obadiah in a tone of obituary. "Sech a coon dog! *Bose!* An' a swimmer! *Bose!* How he used ter drive up the cow! Oh, *Bose!*"

"Ye talk like nobody in the mountings hed a dog but you-uns," panted one of the fleeing hunters. "Ye ought ter be thankful ye air out'n the painter's jaws — 'thout no gun!"

"Oh, Bose ain't no common dog!" cried the bereaved Skimpy; "Bose is like folks! Bose *is* folks!" rising to the apotheosis of grief.

He did not run like folks. Deserted both by boys and dogs he had bravely encountered the panther. It required not only a broken rib and repeated grips of the creature's teeth, but the stealthy approach of its mate to convince Bose how grievously he was overmatched. Then this gifted dog, whose prowess was only exceeded by his intelligence, saw that it was time to run. He passed the boys with the action of a canine meteor. He sought the seclusion beneath the house and he did not leave it for days.

When Ike struck into the road that leads by Keedon Bluffs he was feeling considerably nettled by the result of the adventure, and resolved that hereafter he would always carry a gun for any presumable panther that might hang upon the outskirts of a coon-hunt. He walked on slowly for a time, sure that the panther would hardly follow so far, if indeed she had followed at all. He listened now and then, hearing no sound of the hunt or of the hunters. It was growing late, he knew as he glanced at the sky. The moon had risen high — a waning moon of a lustrous reddish tint, sending long shafts of yellow light down the dusky woods, and, despite its brightness, of grewsome and melancholy suggestions. As the road turned he came upon the great Bluffs towering above the river, and he noted the spherical amber reflection in the dark current below, with trailing lines of light and gilded ripples seeming to radiate from it. A vague purple nullity had blurred the familiar distances, but close at hand all was wonderfully distinct. The gloomy forest on one side of the road drew a sharp summit line along the sky. A blackberry bush, denuded of all but a few leaves, was not more definite than the brambly wands of its shadow on the sandy road. As he drew nearer he noted how dark the water was, how white in the slant of the yellow moonlight rose the great sheer sandstone Bluffs; how black, how distinct were the cavities in the rock. And the voiceless beams played about the old cannon-ball on the ledge. How silent! Only his crunching tread, half muffled in the soft sand; the almost imperceptible murmur of the deep waters; the shrilling of a cricket somewhere, miraculously escaped from the frost. Near midnight, it must have been. He realized how tired he was. He suddenly sat down on the verge of the Bluffs, his feet dangling over, and leaned his back against a bowlder behind him.

He drew a long sigh of fatigue and gazed meditatively below. The next moment he gave a quick start. There along the ledges and niches of the great Bluffs, climbing down diagonally with the agility of a cat, was a dark figure, that at the instant he could hardly recognize as beast or man — or might it be some mysterious being that the cavities of the rock harbored! As he remembered the stories of the witches of Keedon Bluffs, which he had flouted and scorned, he felt a cold thrill quiver through every limb.

A sharp exclamation escaped his lips. Instantly he saw the climbing creature give a great start and then stand still as if with responsive fright. He bent forward and strained his eyes.

He had not yet recovered his normal pulse; his heart was still plunging with wild throbs; nevertheless he noted keenly every movement of the strange object, and as it turned in the direction whence came the intrusive voice, it looked up apprehensively. Ike said nothing, but gazed down into the pallid face lifted in the white moonlight.

VIII.

"Hello!" cried out the figure.

"Hello! — hello! — hello!" the echoing voices of Keedon Bluffs sepulchrally hailed the boy.

Now Ike would have been indignant had some one suspected him of being afraid of the witches of the Bluffs. But he was immensely relieved by this form of address. For although he had never held intimate converse with witches he felt sure they did not say "Hello!"

He leaned over and responded in a sturdy tone "Hello, yerse'f!"

"Hello yerse'f!" cried out the prompt echoes. Ike drew back a little. Although he had acquitted the climbing man of being a witch, he could not repulse an odd uncomfortable feeling that scores of mischievous invisible spirits of the rock were assisting at the conversation. He could imagine that they nudged each other as they repeated the words.

Perhaps they all fell to silently laughing when a belated voice far down the river called in a doubtful and hesitant tone, "Hello yerse'f!"

"Who's that up thar?" demanded the man, still looking up.

"Ike Guyther," the boy replied.

He could not accurately distinguish the sound, so confused was he by the iteration of the meddlesome echoes, but it seemed to him that the man uttered a sudden gruff imprecation at the revelation of his name, and surely the tell-tale rocks were presently grumbling in an uncertain and displeased undertone.

Ike strained his eyes to recognize the features, but the man looked down suddenly and coughed dubiously.

There was something vaguely familiar in his voice that might have served to establish his identity but for the repetitious sounds that followed every word.

"What air ye doin' up thar?" demanded the man, and all the echoes became inquisitorial.

"Been a-coon-huntin'. What ye doin' down thar?" said Ike, at last thinking it but fair that he should ask a few questions himself.

The white face was once more turned downward, and the man coughed and seemed to try to spit out his doubt. It had evidently not occurred to him that he himself was unrecognized, for with a tone that indicated that he sought to make the best of an awkward situation he said, "Why, I hearn Ab talkin' wunst in a while 'bout climbin' down Keedon Bluffs, ter that old cannon-ball on that ledge, an' I 'lowed I'd try ef the thing could be done — jes' fur fun — ha! ha! Toler'ble tough fun, though."

The vain effort at jollity, the strained nervous tone, the merciless echoes exaggerated a thousand fold. But Ike Guyther sat unheeding, more perturbed than he could well have expressed.

It was Jerry Binwell, his father's guest. How had he escaped, Ike wondered, from the roof room where his host thought he lay sleeping? Had he stolen out from amongst the unconscious family, leaving the doors ajar that any marauder might enter? He could not. Old Hiram slept as lightly as a cat, and the blind man was often wakeful and restless. And what could be his object here in the stealthy midnight, risking life and limb — nay, neither! Ike Guyther, watching him climbing — with the frightful depths below into which a false step would instantly precipitate him — lost that morbid and nervous fascination which a feat of great danger induces in the spectator, and began suddenly to experience a sort of confidence, merging into certainty. He was amazed at the lightness, the strength, the marvelous elasticity, the fine precision of every movement. Strain credulity as he might, he could not believe Binwell when he said suddenly, "But I ain't goin' ter try it enny furder — break my neck! This hyar chicken is a-gittin' old an' stiff; couldn't git down thar ter save my life."

He climbed up and up, his silent shadow climbing with him till he neared the spot where Ike sat, when he suddenly paused.

"Git up, Ike," he said; "that's the only place whar thar's purchase enough ter pull up by."

He evidently knew all the ground. Ike dragged himself out of the way, and, with his hands in his pockets, stood pensively watching him as he pulled himself to the verge, and then upon his knees, and so to his feet on the roadside. He paused for a moment, panting. He looked at his companion with an expression which had no relation to the words on his lips. Many a boy might not have detected this yawning gulf between what he meant and what he said, but Ike's senses were sharpened by suspicion and anxiety.

"Whew! Great Molly Har'!" Jerry mopped his brow with his red cotton handkerchief. "I'm too old fur sech didoes as this hyar — old man's a-goin' fas'. Knees plumb bent. Don't ye laff, Ike! Don't ye laff." Ike had shown no sign of merriment. "An' 'fore everything don't ye tell Ab ez I tried ter climb down Keedon Bluffs ter that old ball, an' could n't. I would n't hev the mounting ter git a-holt o' that thar joke on me fur nuthin'!"

He looked sharply at the boy, who said not a word, but simply stared at him as he stood on the verge of the Bluff in the slanting melancholy yellow light of the waning moon. There was a quiver in Binwell's nostril, a nervous motion of the lips, a keen inimical gleam of the eyes under his hat brim. He was giving Ike more notice than he had ever before bestowed on him.

"Hey!" he cried jocularly, clapping the boy on the shoulder, "don't ye tell on me, Ike — ye won't, will ye?"

This direct appeal brought an answer. But Ike was on his guard.

"Mebbe then uncle Ab would quit thinkin' ez how *he* could," he said cautiously.

Jerry Binwell suddenly changed his tactics.

"Tell ennybody ye want ter, ye wide-mouthed shoat, ye! Ef I can't climb down thar nobody else kin, an' nobody air a-goin' ter try. Got too tender feelin's fur thar necks. I ain't ashamed o' gittin' old nohow! Ye'll be whar I am some day, Ike, ef ye don't die fust."

He strode on ahead with a deft free step. Ike, doubtful and grievously ill at ease, followed. Come what might he felt that he would tell his father all, and let him solve the mystery about this strange guest. Then he began to reflect how slight this "all" was. There were the innuendoes of the men at the store; but his father knew as well as he how little Jerry Binwell had been liked in his early youth, how strong the prejudice remained. The affront to old Corbin was indeed reprehensible, but as to climbing about the rocks at night surely any one might do that who was foolish or idle or nimble enough.

Ike was surprised that although he found in summing up there was no positive heinous wickedness involved, his aversion to the man remained and his resolution was strong. He would tell his father all that he had heard, that he had seen. He would shift the responsibility. His shoulders were not strong enough to carry it.

Jerry's long, lean figure, with the company of his longer and leaner shadow which dogged his steps like some pursuing phantom of sorrow or dismay that might materialize in the fullness of time, kept steadily down the road. He made no pretense of silence or concealment, but whistled blithely and loud — a sound to pierce the pensive hour with discordant interruption. Did it awaken the birds? A peevish, intermittent chirring rose drowsily from the woods, and then was still, and anon sounded again. Or was it that the dawn was coming hardily upon the slowly departing night, long lingering, loath to go? The moon showed no paling sign; belts of pearly vapors, catching its light, were rising from the furthest reaches of the purple mountains. And here the river was dark and deep; and there it flowed in translucent amber waves, with a silver flash of foam, all the brighter for the shadow of the rock hard by. And now it was out of sight and there were the long stretches of the familiar woods on either hand, with no suggestion of the vivid tints of autumn, only a dusky black alternating with a gleaming gold strewn like the largess of a dream fantasy all a-down the winding ways. .

THE STORY OF KEEDON BLUFFS. 129

Morning surely; the thrush sings a stave. And silence again.

The shadows falter, though the pensive lunar light yet lingers. And again the thrush — fresh, thrilling, a quiver of ecstasies, a soaring wing, though it catches the yellow moonbeams. The sky reddens. Alas, for the waning moon! Oh, sorry ghost; how pale! how pale!

For the prosaic day is in the awakening woods. The mountains rise above their encompassing mists and shadows. Beneath them, brown and gray, with closed batten shutters, Ike sees, slowly revealed, his father's house, the sheep lying huddled at one side, barely astir — a head lifted now, and then dropped — the cow drowsing in a fence corner; the chickens beginning to jump down from the althea bushes, where, despite the autumnal chill, they still roost. And, as the first slanting sun ray shoots up over the mountains, the door opens, and there is thrust out the pink face of Rosamond, dimpling with glee at the sight of them, and her shout of glad recognition is loud enough to waken all the sluggards in the cabin, or for that matter in the Cove.

The cabin, however, was already astir. Ike learned, with emotions not altogether relating to the recital, that his father's aunt who had brought him up from infancy had been taken ill, and a runner having been sent to apprise him he had gone over to the Carolina side, and would not return until the old woman should be better or the worst over.

Ike had postponed his disclosures too long. There was little good, he thought, as he swung his axe at the wood-pile — as wide awake as though he had participated in no coon-hunt — to tell his mother; she had cares enough — and what could she do? And truly he had nothing to tell except to put into words vague suspicions; nay, his thoughts were not so well defined; to canvass actions and accents and looks that displeased him. They all knew — at least they would not be surprised to learn that Jerry Binwell had not outlived the malice of his youth. Aunt Jemima would regard the slightest word against him as an effort to bereave her of this late-blooming pleasure and joy of her life, the little Rosamond. Ike hopefully considered for a time the blind man's aversion to Binwell. Abner would never hear nor reply when he spoke — and since the first night, he had not spoken to Binwell, except indeed one day when he chanced to stumble against the sprawling loafer before the fire. Abner struck at him fiercely and called out imperiously — " Get out of my way — or I will kick you out !"

Jerry had moved, but there was an odd glancing expression from his half-closed lids that alarmed Ike, so malignant it seemed. The little girl had run gayly up, caught Abner by the hand, and guided him to his place by the fire. For she it was who had superseded all the others, and had made the blind artillery-man her special charge. All day she was laughing beside him. Any time the oddly assorted couple could be met, she leading him carefully, holding two of his bronzed fingers, as they strolled down the sunset road, or they might be seen sitting on the wood-pile while he told her stories or sang. And she sang also, loud and clear — gayly too, whatever might have been the humble poet's mood — in no wise dismayed or hindered by the infantile disability of not being able to carry a tune. She had a thousand quirks and conceits, incredibly entertaining to him in his enforced idleness. She had watched wide-eyed when Hiram Guyther read from an old and tattered Testament, for the accomplishment of reading was rare in the region, and had not before been brought to her observation. Often thereafter she equipped herself with a chip, held sturdily before her dancing eyes, and from this unique book she droned forth, in imitation of Hiram's gruff voice, strange stories of beasts and birds, and the human beings about her, pausing only to scream with laughter at her own wit, and then gruffly droned on once more. She fell ill once for a day or so — a red and a swollen throat, and a flushing, dull-eyed fever. Aunt Jemima and Ike's mother exhausted their skill and simple remedies, and went about haggard and nervous; and the blind man, breaking a long silence, said suddenly, "Ef ennything war ter happen ter that thar child I 'd 'low the Lord hed fursook me."

A neighbor, who happened to be at the house, eyed him curiously. "Ef I war you-uns, Ab," he said, "I 'd 'low ez He hed fursook me whenst He let my eyes git put out."

The brave fellow had had no repinings, not even when the war was his daily thought. Now he seemed to have forgotten it, so full, and varied, and cheerful an interest had this little creature brought into his life. Often aunt Jemima would tell in gladsome superlatives what she looked like, and when she spoke he would turn an intent smiling face toward her as if he beheld some charming image.

What was the use of talking, Ike thought, remembering all this. They would not jeopardize the loan of this treasure for all that Jerry Binwell could do or say.

He cut away vehemently at the wood, making the chips fly and the mountain echoes ring. He responded curtly, but without discourtesy, when Jerry Binwell came out of the house, took a seat upon the wood-pile, and began to talk to him. Jerry had a confidential tone, and he slyly laughed at the folks in the Cove, and he took on a comrade-like manner — implying a certainty of appreciation and sympathy — that might once have flattered Ike, coming from one so much older than himself. Now, however, Ike merely swung the axe in silence, casting an occasional distrustful glance at the thin sharp face with its long grayish goatee. More than once he encountered a keen inquiring look that did not seem to agree with the careless, casual nature of the talk.

"Old Jake Corbin — ye know him; oh yes, ye seen me h'ist him up on the beam thar at the store — waal, he be powerful keen ter get a chance ter torment other folks, but cut a joke on him, an' I tell ye, old Jake 'll git his mad up, sure. I seen him the 'tother day, an' he plumb looked wild-cats at me — fairly glared. Tell ye, Ike, ye an' me 'll git round him some day, an' hev some fun out'n him — git his dander up an' see him hop." He winked at Ike and chewed resolutely on his huge quid of tobacco.

"Naw, I won't," said Ike suddenly. "I hev' been raised ter respec' my elders. An' I'm a-goin' ter do it now jes' the same ez afore ye kem."

"Bless my bones!" cried Jerry Binwell, affecting contemptuous surprise and speaking in a jeering falsetto voice. "Jes' listen how leetle Sally do talk — ye plumb perlite leetle gal!" He leered unpleasantly at the flushing boy. Then he suddenly resumed his natural tone and his former manner, as if he had borne no part in this interlude.

"Ye oughter hear how he talks 'bout you-uns, Ike — 'lows ye air plumb lazy."

"That war a true word whenst he said it," interpolated Ike.

"An' never done yer work, an' war onreliable, an' onstiddy, an' hed n't no grit ter stan' up ter yer word, an' thar war no sech thing ez makin' a man out'n ye. I hearn him say that an' mo', 'fore twenty other men."

Ike's axe had dropped to the ground. He listened with a red cheek and a glowing eye. The other watched him intently.

"Waal, that's pretty tough talk," said Ike.

"'T is *that!*" assented Binwell.

"But I hev been shirking some an' no mistake, an' I reckon the old man 'lowed that war jes' the kind o' stuff I be made out'n, totally. Now I be a-goin' ter show him 't ain't nuthin' more 'n a streak."

And the steady strokes of the axe rang, and the chips flew, and the mountains echoed the industrial sound.

Jerry Binwell looked unaccountably disappointed and disturbed. He changed the subject. "Why war ye axin' Ab fur the loan o' his gun this mornin'?"

"Kase dad hev kerried his'n off, an' I be a-goin' ter git up the boys an' go arter that thar painter. It riles me powerful ter go a-huntin' a coon an' git run by a painter. So I 'lowed we-uns would go ter-night."

Again the man slouching on the wood-pile seemed unaccountably worried and ill at ease. This reminded Ike of that curious nocturnal climbing of the rocks, and when he went up to the roof-room for some lead to mould bullets for the gun, he stood looking about him and wondering how Jerry Binwell contrived to escape from his hospitable quarters without rousing the family who slept in the room and in the shed-room below. There was no window; the long tent-like place was illumined only by the many cracks in the wall and roof. They had a dazzling silvery glister when one looked steadily at the light pouring through them amongst the brown timbers, and the many garments, and bags, and herbs, and peltries, hanging from the ridge-pole. One of these rifts struck him as wider than he had thought any of them could be. He reached up and touched the clapboard. It was loose; it rose with the pressure. A man not half so active as Binwell could have sprung through and upon the roof, and thence swung himself to the ground.

The panther was surprised and killed that night. Jerry Binwell, and several other men who heard of the adventure, joined the party. They were all in high feather going home, and Skimpy sang a number of his roundelays, as he had often done before without exciting any particular admiration. He sang from animal spirits, as the other boys, less musically endowed, shouted and grotesquely yelled. Nevertheless, with the musician's susceptibility to plaudits, his ear was attuned to Jerry Binwell's exclamation, addressed to one of the men in the rear, "Jes' listen how that thar young one kin sing! 'Pears plumb s'prisin'!"

And the good-natured mountaineer returned, "That's a fac'. Wouldn't be s'prised none ef Skimp shows a reg'lar gift fur quirin'."

"He sings better now 'n all the folkses in the church-house," said the guileful Jerry.

The flattered Skimpy!

He knew that the society of Ike had been forbidden to him, lest he should come in contact with this elderly reprobate, but he felt a great flutter of delight when Binwell, coming up beside him, as he trotted along in the moonlight, said again that he could sing like all possessed, and declared that if he had a fiddle he could teach Skimpy many new tunes that he had heard when he lived down in

Persimmon Cove. "Mighty fiddlin' folks down thar," he added, seductively.

Now there was hanging on the wall at the Sawyer house — and it is barely possible that Jerry Binwell may have seen it there — a crazy old fiddle and bow. It was claimed as the property of Obadiah, the eldest of the boys, who had his share of such musical talent as blessed the Sawyer family. In him it expressed itself in fiddling to the exclusion of his brothers — for very intolerant was he of anybody who undertook to "play the fool with this fiddle," as he phrased it. A critical person might have said that he played the fool with it himself, or perhaps that it played the fool with him. But such as the performance was, he esteemed the instrument as the apple of his eye, and was very solicitous of not breaking its "bredge." Therefore Skimpy was a very bold boy, and preposterously hopeful, when he suggested to Binwell that he could borrow Obadiah's fiddle, and thus the treasures of sound so rapturously fiddled forth by the dwellers in Persimmon Cove might rejoice the air in Tanglefoot.

"Naw, naw, don't 'sturb Obadiah," said the considerate Jerry. "Jes' to-morrer evenin', two hours by sun, whenst he ain't needin' it an' ain't studyin' bout'n it, ye jes' git it, an' ye kem an' meet me by the sulphur spring, an' I kin l'arn ye them new chunes."

Skimpy's ridiculous attenuated shadow thumped along in front of them; Jerry's eyes were fixed upon it — he was too cautious to scan the boy himself. It stumped its toe presently on a stone which Skimpy was too much absorbed to see, and so it had to hop and limp for a while. Skimpy said nothing, for he was wondering how it would be easiest and safest to undertake to play the fool with that fiddle of Obadiah's.

They were a considerable distance in advance of the others and nearing Keedon Bluffs; the whoopings of their invisible companions, who were hidden by the frequent turns in the road, came now and again upon the air, arousing the latent voices of the rocks; occasionally there was only the sound of loud indistinguishable talking, as if the powers of the earth and the air had broken out in prosaic communion.

"Pipe up, sonny," said the paternal Jerry, seeing that the conversation was not likely to be resumed. "Gin us that one bout'n 'Dig Taters;' that thar one air new ter me."

To his surprise Skimpy refused. "I can't 'pear ter git no purchase on it hyar. Them rocks keep up sech a hollerin'."

They trudged on in silence for a few minutes. Then said Skimpy, glancing back over his shoulder, "I wish them boys would stir thar stumps an' overhaul us. I hate ter be with sech a few folks arter night-fall 'roun Keedon Bluffs," — he shrank apprehensively from the verge.

"What fur?" demanded Jerry sharply.

"Kase," Skimpy lowered his voice and slipped nearer to his companion, "the folkses 'low ez thar be witches 'round hyar of a night arter it gits cleverly dark an' lays by day in them hollows in the Bluffs, an' kem out of a night ter strangle folkses." He suddenly remembered from whom he had heard these fables. "Ye know 't war *you-uns* ez war a-tellin' me an' Ike 'bout them witches fus' evenin' we ever seen ye — along this hyar road with yer kyart an' yer leetle gal."

Binwell was silent for a moment. Then he began to laugh in a chuckling way, and the Bluffs responded in muffled and sinister merriment. "'T war jes' a pack o' lies, Skimp!" he said jovially. " I jes' done it ter skeer that thar boy ez war along o' you-uns — Ike Guyther. He be powerful easy skeered, an' I wanted ter see how he'd look! I tell ye of a night he jes' gathers his bones tergether an' sets close ter the ha'th. Ef enny witches take arter him, they'll hev ter kem down the chimbly afore all the fambly. Ike, he puts them witches on thar mettle ter ketch him."

"Waal, sir!" exclaimed the candid Skimpy, "it skeered me a sight wuss 'n it did Ike. I 'lowed I'd never git home; ef I hed hed ez many feet ez a thousand-legs I could hev fund a use fur 'em all. An' them two I did hev mos' weighed a ton. Ike never 'peared ter me ter skeer a speck."

There was no doubt in his tones. He was a friendly fellow himself, and he looked only for fair-dealing in others.

"Waal, I never went ter skeer *you-uns*," said Jerry in his companionable manner. "I seen from the fust jes' what sort'n boy you-uns war — stiddy, an' reliable, an' the kind o' feller ez a body kin put dependence in — know jes' whar ter find ye."

Skimpy listened in tingling delight to this sketch — it would not have been recognized at home. His mother might have considered it ridicule.

"I jes' wanted ter skeer that thar t'other boy " — he was looking Skimpy over very closely as he spoke, his eyes narrowing, his lips pursed up in a sort of calculation — he might have seemed to be mentally measuring Skimpy's attenuated frame. "I jes' wanted ter skeer that thar t'other boy. He's powerful mean, Ike is. He air always a-purtendin' ter like ennybody, an' then a-laffin' at 'em ahint thar backs. I did n't know him then, but I knowed his uncle Ab, an' I seen the minit I clapped eyes on him ez they war jes' alike. An' ez I hed a reason fur it, I skeered him. He's mighty cantankerous ahint ennybody's back," Jerry continued as he strode on, swinging his right arm. "I hev hearn him declar' ez that thar old cur o' yourn, Bose, air the bes'-lookin' member o' the Sawyer fambly." He glanced sharply at Skimpy, steadily stumping along the sandy road.

"Waal, ye know," said Skimpy in a high excited voice, "Bose, ye know, is a plumb special coon-dog. An' he's sharp; mighty few gyard-dogs sech ez Bose. An' he air a shepherd too. I'll be bound none o' our sheep air ever missin' or kilt. An' Bose sets ez much store by the baby ez enny o' the fambly do; he jes' gyards that cradle; he'll snap at me if I so much ez kem nigh it — nobody but mam kin tech that baby arter Bose takes his stand. An' Bose, he kin go out an' find our cow out 'n fifty an' fetch her home."

Binwell had long ago perceived that he had touched the wrong chord. Skimpy was quite content to be rated as secondary in beauty to the all-accomplished and beloved Bose.

"I know Bose," he admitted. "Bose is hard to beat."

"*Yes*, sir! Yes, *sir!*" And Skimpy wagged his convinced head.

"But Ike 'lows he be ugly."

"Shucks! I say ugly!" cried Skimpy scornfully; he was willing to be considered no beauty himself — but *Bose!*

"An' he 'lows he 'd jes' ez lief hear Bose howl ez you-uns sing."

Skimpy paused, turning his astonished face up to Binwell, the moonlight full upon its stung and indignant expression. Now Bose had never been considered musical — not even by Skimpy. He drew the line that bounds perfection at Bose's dulcet utterances. He was almost incredulous at this, despite his confiding nature.

"Why, I hev jes' sot an' sung fur Ike till I mighty nigh los' my breath."

"Ye oughter hear him mock ye, arter ye gits gone. Oh, Mister Coon! Oh, e-aw, Mister Kyune!" mimicked Jerry in an insulting falsetto. "He 'lows it gin him the year-ache; ye 'members how bad he had it."

"Dellaw!" exclaimed the outdone and amazed Skimpy, stopping in the road, his breath short, his face scarlet.

"Made me right up an' down mad," said Jerry. "Oh, I knowed that Ike, minit I set eyes on him! I knowed his deceivin' natur'. I wanted ter skeer him away from Keedon Bluffs. I never minded you-uns. I'd jes' ez lief tell you-uns ez not why I wanted ter keep him off'n 'em."

"What fur?" said Skimpy, once more trudging along.

"Waal, hyar I be whar my road turns off from yer road," said Jerry, pausing. He stood at the forks of the road, half in the light of the moon, half in the shadow of the thinning overhanging foliage. The mists were in the channel of the river, and the banks were brimming with the lustrous pearly floods; the blue sky was clear save that the moon was beset by purple broken clouds — all veined about with opalescent gleams. The shadows were black in the woods; the long shafts of light, yellow and slanting, penetrated far down the aisles, which seemed very lonely and silent; an acorn presently fell from the chestnut oak above Binwell's head into the white sandy road, so unfrequented that the track of a wagon which had passed long before would hardly be soon displaced unless by the wind or the rain.

"I tell ye," said Jerry, looking down into the candid upturned face beneath the torn brim of the old white wool hat, "ye fetch Obadiah's fiddle ter-morrer, an hour 'fore sundown, ter the sulphur spring, an' I'll l'arn ye them new chunes. An' I'll tell ye all 'bout Ike, an' what he said an' why I wanter keep sech ez him off'n them Bluffs."

"Waal," assented Skimpy, "I kin make out ter git the fiddle, I reckon."

But it was with little joyous anticipation that he turned away. Ike's words, as reported by Binwell, rankled in his heart; it was hot and heavy within him. He even shed a forlorn tear or two — to thus make acquaintance with the specious delusions of friendship. It was not so much the sting of wounded vanity, although he was sensible too of this — but that Ike should affect to esteem him so dearly and ridicule him behind his back! He was generous enough, however, to seek to make excuses to himself for his friend. "I reckon," he muttered, "it mus' hev been arter dad would n't lemme go with Ike no mo' an' it riled him, an' so he tuk ter tongue-lashin' me. I reckon he never thunk ez I could n't holp it."

And thus he disappeared down the woodland ways, leaving Jerry Binwell standing in the road and looking meditatively after him.

"I reckon it's better ennyhow," Binwell soliloquized. "Ike's a hundred times smarter 'n him, but he air smart enuff. Bes' not be *too* smart. An' though he be ez tall ez Ike he's a deal stringier; he's powerful slim. Ike ain't much less 'n me — an' I be a deal too bulky — git stuck certain. Skimpy 's the boy."

He remained silent for a time, vacantly gazing down the woods. Then suddenly he turned and betook himself homeward.

IX.

CIRCUMSTANCES the next day seemed adverse to Skimpy's scheme. Obadiah for some time past had not been musically disposed, and the violin had hung silent on the cabin wall in company with strings of red peppers, and bags of herbs, and sundry cooking utensils. That afternoon the spirit of melody within him was newly awakened.

Skimpy, who had been lurking about the place, watching his opportunity, was dismayed to see Obadiah come briskly out of the cabin door with the instrument in his hand, and establish himself in a rickety chair on the porch. He tilted this back on its hind-legs until he could lean against the wall, stuck the violin under his chin, and with his long lean arm in a fascinating crook, he began to bow away rapturously. They were very merry tunes that Obadiah played — at least the tempo was lively and required a good many quick jerks and nods of the head, and much flirting and shaking of his long red mane to keep up with it. Occasionally his bow would glance off the strings with a very dashing effect, when he would hold it at arm's-length, and grin with satisfaction, and wink triumphantly at Skimpy, who had come and seated himself on the steps of the porch hard by. He looked up from under the wide brim of his hat somewhat wistfully at Obadiah.

The violinist was happier for an audience, although he could have sat alone till sunset, with one leg doubled up under the other, which swayed loosely from the tilted elevation of the chair, and played for his own appreciative ear, and found art sufficient unto itself. But applause is a pleasant concomitant of proficiency and he loved to astonish Skimpy. His hat had fallen on the floor, and the kitten, fond of queer places to sleep, had coiled herself in the crown, and now and then lifted her head and looked out dubiously at Skimpy. Just above Obadiah was a shelf on which stood a pail of water and a gourd. What else there was up there an inquisitive young rooster was trying to find out, having flown over the heedless musician, still blithely sawing away.

"He oughter hev his wings cropped, so ez he couldn't fly around that a-way," said Skimpy suddenly. "Oughtn't he, Oby?"

Now one would imagine that when Obadiah was harmoniously disposed all the chords of his nature would be attuned to the fine consonance which so thrilled him. On the contrary the vibrations of his temper were most discordant when his mood was most melodic. He had one curt effective rejoinder for any remark that might seek to interrupt him.

"Hesh up!" he said, tartly.

His mother, a tall gaunt woman of an aggressively neat appearance, was hanging out the clothes to dry on the althea bushes in the sun. She was near enough to overhear the conversation, and she suddenly joined in it.

"Nobody oughter want ter tie up other folkses tongues till they be right sure they hev got no call ter be tongue-tied tharself."

To this reproof Obadiah refrained from making any unfilial reply, but scraped away joyously till Skimpy, longing for silence and the fiddle, felt as if the mountains shimmering through the haze were beginning to clumsily dance, and experienced a serious difficulty in keeping his own feet still, so nervous had he become in his eagerness to lay hold of the bow himself.

Sunset would be kindling presently — he gazed anxiously toward the western sky across the vast landscape, for the cabin was perched well up on the mountain slope, and the privilege of overlooking the long stretches of valley and range and winding river was curtailed only by the limits of vision. The sun was as yet a glittering focus of dazzling white rays, but they would be reddening soon, and doubtless his new friend was already waiting for him at the sulphur spring.

"I wisht ye'd lemme hev that thar fiddle a leetle while, Oby," he said suddenly, his manner at once beguiling for the sake of the favor he sought, and reproachful for the denial he foresaw.

Obadiah's arm seemed electrified — there was one terrific shriek from the cat-gut, and then his quivering hand held the bow silent above the strings.

"Air ye turned a bodacious idjit, Skimp?" he cried, positively appalled by the audacity of the request. "I would n't hev ye a-ondertakin' ter play the fool with this hyar fiddle, fur" — he hesitated, but his manner swept away worlds of entreating bribes — "fur *nuthin'*."

The young rooster, finding that there was nothing upon the shelf except the water-pail and gourd, and hardly caring to appropriate them, had made up his mind to descend. After the manner of his kind, however, he teetered about on the edge of the shelf in some excitement, unable to determine just at what spot to attempt the leap. Twice or thrice he spread his bronzed red and yellow wings, stretched his neck, and bowed his body down — to rise up exactly where he was before. At last the adventurous fowl decided to trust himself to providence. With a squawk at his own temerity he fluttered awkwardly off the shelf, and almost alighted on the musician's head, giving a convulsive clutch at it with his claws as he flopped past. There was a distressful whine from the fiddle-strings in Obadiah's sudden perversion of the bow; he had forgotten all about the rooster on the shelf; he jumped back with a galvanic jerk, as he felt the fluttering wings about his head and the scrape of the yellow claws, and emitted a sharp cry of startled dismay.

Bose, who had been lying close beside a clumsy wooden box on rockers, growled surlily, fixing a warning eye on the boy; then his voice rose into a gruff bark. There was no longer use in his keeping quiet and guarding the cradle. Beneath the quilts was a great commotion; the personage enveloped therein, although sleeping according to infantile etiquette with its head covered, had no mind to be thus eclipsed when broad awake. There presently emerged a pair of mottled fists, the red head of the Sawyer tribe, an indignant, frowning red face, and a howl so vigorous that it seemed almost visible. It had no accompaniment of tears, for the baby wept for rage rather than grief, and sorrow was the share of those who heard him.

Mrs. Sawyer turned and looked reproachfully at the group on the porch.

"'T war n't *me*, mam, 't war the rooster ez woke the baby," Obadiah exclaimed, seeking to exculpate himself.

Bose was stretching himself to a surprising length, all his toe-nails elongated as he spread out his paws, and still half-growling and half-barking at Obadiah, the utterance complicated with a yawn.

"'T war the rooster," reiterated Obadiah — "the rooster, an' — an' — Bose."

"'T war n't Bose!" exclaimed Skimpy, loyally.

"Hesh up!" said the dulcet musician.

"Need n't tell me nuthin' ag'in Bose — I know Bose!" said Mrs. Sawyer emphatically — thus a good name is ever proof against detraction. "Hang up that thar fiddle, Oby," she continued. "I wonder the baby ain't been woked up afore considerin' the racket ye kep' up. An' go down yander ter the 'tater patch an' see ef yer dad don't need ye ter holp dig the 'taters. I don't need ye hyar—an' that fiddle don't need ye nuther. I be half crazed with that thar everlastin' sawin' an' scrapin' o' yourn, keepin' on ez ef yer muscles war witched, an' ye *could n't* quit."

She sat down on a chair beside the cradle and began to rock it with her foot, readjusting the while the quilts over the head of the affronted infant, who straightway flung them off again that he might have more room for his vocalization.

Obadiah went obediently and hung up the fiddle, and presently looking down the slope Skimpy saw him wending his way toward the potato patch.

"I dunno how kem Oby 'lows that thar old fiddle b'longs to him, more 'n it do ter the rest o' we-uns," Skimpy observed discontentedly, when the baby's vociferations had subsided into a sort of soliloquy, keeping time with the rhythmic motions of the rockers. It was neither mutter nor wail nor indicative of unhappiness, but it expressed a firmly perverse resolution not to go to sleep again if he could help it, and rose instantly into a portentous howl if the monotonous rocking was intermitted for a moment.

" 'T war yer gran'dad's fiddle," said Mrs. Sawyer. "That's the only sure enough owner it ever hed — he never gin it ter nobody in partic'lar whenst he died. An' it jes' hung thar on the wall till Obadiah 'peared ter take a kink ter play it."

Obadiah doubtless considered himself entitled to the fiddle by the right of primogeniture — though Obadiah did not call it by this name. As Skimpy reflected upon the nature of his brother's claim he felt that there was no reason why he should not insist on sharing the ownership. It was not Obadiah's fiddle — it belonged to the family.

The baby's voice sank gradually to a jerky monotone, then to a murmur and so to silence. The rockers of the cradle jogged thumpingly up and down the floor for a few minutes longer. And then Mrs. Sawyer betook herself once more to her task of hanging out the clothes, while Bose guarded the cradle, and Skimpy still sat on the steps, his elbows on his knees, and his pondering head held between his hands.

The lengthening yellow sunbeams poured through the cabin door, venturing gradually up the walls to where the silent instrument hung, filling it with a rich glow and playing many a fantasy though never stirring a string.

X.

WHEN Jerry Binwell repaired to the sulphur spring that afternoon, there was no waiting figure amongst the rocks beside it. He paused at a little distance and glanced about with surprise. Then he slouched on toward the trysting place. In all the long avenues of the woods that seemed illumined by the clear amber tint of the dead leaves covering the ground, on which the dark boles of the trees stood out with startling distinctness, his roving eye encountered no living creature, except indeed a squirrel. It was perched upright upon the flat slab that almost hid the spring, eating a chestnut held between its deft paws; it scudded away, its curling tail waving as it ran up a tree hard by, and Binwell heard it chattering there afterward; more than once it dropped empty nutshells upon the man's hat as he waited half-reclining among the rocks beside the spring. Time dawdled on ; the sunshine adjusted itself to a new slant; it deepened to a richer tint; the shadows became pensive; the squirrel had fled long ago. Often Binwell lifted himself on his elbow and glanced about him, frowning surlily; but the vast woods were utterly solitary and very still this quiet day. Once a rustling sound caught his ear, and as he sprang up looking about hopefully for the boy, his motion alarmed some hogs that were roaming wild in the forest to fatten on the mast. They stood still, and fixed small sharp eyes intently upon him, then with an exclamatory and distrustful vociferation they ran off through the woods hardly less fleetly than deer. Jerry Binwell muttered his discontent, and glancing once more at the sky began to walk slowly about, keeping the spring in sight. Still no Skimpy came. The man's face wore an expression both scornful and indignant as he paused at last.

The forest was remarkably free from undergrowth just here; the fiery besoms of the annual conflagrations destroyed the young and tender shoots, and left to the wilderness something of the aspect of a vast park. Only on one side, and that was where the ground sloped suddenly to the depths of a rugged ravine, an almost impenetrable jungle of laurel reached from the earth into the branches of the trees. Its ever-green leaves had a summer suggestion as the sun glanced upon them; none had changed, none had fallen. And yet, as he looked, he noted a thinning aspect, a sort of gap at a certain point in the massive wall of interlacing boughs, made, he fancied, when some lumbering bear tore a breach in search of winter quarters in those bosky securities. He was an idle man, and trifles were wont to while away his time. His momentary curiosity served to mitigate the tedium of waiting for Skimpy. He slowly strolled toward the gap amidst the foliage, wondering whether the animal had only lately passed, whether it was possible to come upon it in its lair and surprise it. He was near enough to lay his hand on the laurel leaves when he noticed there was a distinctly marked path threading its way through the tangle. He could not see the ground, but a furrow amongst the boughs indicated continual passing and repassing.

For a few yards this was visible as he stood looking through the gap of bent and broken branches; then the rift among the leaves seemed to curve and he saw no further. Still meditating on the bear, he experienced some surprise when he observed in the marshy earth in the open space near where he stood the print of a man's boot; not his own, as he was half-inclined to think at first. For as he held his foot above the track, he saw that the print in the moist earth was much broader, and that the man walked with a short pace, far different from his own long stride. The steps had not only gone into the laurel but had come thence; often, too, judging from the number and direction of the footprints.

"I wonder whar this path leads," he said. "Somebody must be moonshinin' hyarabouts."

He stood gazing down meditatively. The broad footprint was always the same, the step always the short measure indicating a slow and heavy man.

This suggested the idea of old Corbin. The retort, in the nature of a practical joke, played on the old codger at the store, had not altogether satisfied Binwell's enmity; this, in fact, was, in a measure, reinforced by the surly silence and looks of aversion which had since been meted out to him throughout the community. It was more than curiosity which he now felt; it was a certain joy in secretly spying upon his enemy, and there was a merry sneer in his eyes as he began to push his way through the laurel. As the path curved, he saw the groove among the leaves anew before him, and he had but to follow its twists and turns. A long way it led him down the rugged descent, the laurel leaves almost closing over his head, the great forest trees rising high above the thicket, flinging their darkling shadows into the midst. He was chuckling to think what a time of it old Corbin must have had to get down. "An' how in Kingdom Come did he ever git up ag'in?" he laughed.

The words had hardly escaped his lips before he emitted a husky cry of surprise: he had come suddenly to his journey's end. In the midst of a clear patch of rocky ground, where even the sturdy laurel could not strike root, were scattered shavings and bits of wood, and stretching into the dense growth, so long they were, lay two staunch but slender poles upon the ground. They were joined by rungs, well fitted in a workman-like manner. It was in fact a great ladder, the like of which had never been seen in Tanglefoot Cove, and, indeed, rarely elsewhere. It might have reached from the river bank to the hollows of Keedon Bluffs! As Binwell gazed with starting eyes he noted that it was nearly completed — only a few rungs remained to be set in.

A sudden vibrating sound set all the stillness to jarring; he turned abruptly, his nerves tense, an oath between his teeth. It was too late for him to hide, to flee. He could only gaze in despair at Skimpy's red head, his white wool hat set on the back of it, bobbing along through the laurel; his freckled, grinning face was bowed on Obadiah's fiddle that wailed and complained beneath his sawing arm.

Perhaps it was the urgency of the moment

that made Binwell bold and rallied his quick expedients. He did not even wonder how the boy had happened to discover him. Skimpy had descried him from a distance in the open woods, and had followed, bringing the fiddle according to their agreement. Binwell looked gravely at the boy and motioned to him to advance. The fiddle ceased to shiver beneath Skimpy's inharmonious touch, and with his eyes stretched, and his mouth too, for that matter, he pressed on down to the spot. He could not restrain a wondering "Waal, sir!" when Binwell pointed to the ladder.

"Don't say nuthin', Skimp," said Binwell. "Lay the fiddle an' bow thar in the laurel; level em' so ez they won't fall; thar! Ye kin find 'em ag'in by that thar rock. Now take a-holt of that thar ladder, 'bout hyar; that's the dinctum — an' jes' foller me."

Skimpy recognized this as an odd proceeding, and yet he hardly felt warranted in questioning Jerry Binwell. He could not refuse his assistance in a mere matter of "toting"; he began to think that this service was the reason his friend had appointed this place of meeting on pretext of playing the fiddle. He did not definitely suspect anything worse than a scheme to get a little unrequited work from him. More especially were his doubts annulled by the quiet glance with which Jerry Binwell met his eager inquiring look.

"Yes, take a-holt right thar" — as if this was an answer to all that the boy was about to ask. Binwell himself had run swiftly ahead and had caught up the other extremity of the ladder. He went straight forward, breaking a path through the jungle by the aid of the ladder that he allowed to precede him by ten or twelve feet. He did not hesitate, although there was no rift here amongst the leaves to guide him. His manner was as assured as if he were following a definite route that he had traveled often. Skimpy had no doubt that he knew whither he was going through that trackless desert. Nevertheless Binwell now and then looked back over his shoulder at the sun, as if to make sure of the direction which he was taking. He did not care to notice the anxious freckled face, down the vista of the leaves, from which all jocundity had vanished. For Skimpy, although the best-natured of boys, began to rebel inwardly. He had a troublous consciousness that Jerry Binwell would not be safe to trust, and wondered that he could have so disregarded his father's wish that he should not be brought into this association. It seemed odd to Skimpy that the danger should have manifested itself so close upon the heels of the warning. In common with many boys, he was apt to regard the elders as too cautious, too slow. He had not learned as yet that it is experience which has made them so. It was not merely mentally that he was ill at ease. His bare feet were beginning to burn, for they had now climbed long distances up the mountain slope amidst the laurel. The weight of the ladder asserted itself in every straining muscle, and yet he realized that his callow strength would hardly have enabled him to carry one end, were it not for the aid of the upholding boughs of the laurel, that would not suffer it to touch the ground, even when his grasp sometimes relaxed in spite of himself. He dreaded to think how he would fare when they should emerge into the open woods. "I won't tote my e-end no furder," he said to himself, still striving to look upon himself as a free agent.

He called once or twice to Binwell, who feigned not to hear. His deafness suddenly vanished when Skimpy stopped and the ladder lay upon the interlacing laurel-boughs. "Whar be we-uns a-goin' ter tote this hyar contrivance, ennyways?" the boy demanded.

"Jes' a leetle furder, sonny," said Jerry Binwell paternally, turning upon him a quiet face, immovable save for the industriously ruminant jaws, subduing a great quid of tobacco; he was apparently so unaware of any cause for suspicions that they were erased from Skimpy's mind. He took up his end of the ladder again, thinking it probably belonged to Binwell, and thankful that he had put into words no intimation of his vague but uneasy doubts. He even hummed a song as he stumped along, willing enough to be cheerful if the adventure only signified a little work for no pay. "But I'd hev ruther not l'arn them chunes folks fiddle down in Persimmon Cove ef I hed knowed I hed ter skitter up the mounting this-a-way."

For they were in truth near the summit, not ascending the great bald, but in a gap between two peaks. The laurel had given way to open woods, and Skimpy's end of the ladder almost dragged. The trees, instead of the great forest kings on the mountain slopes below, were the stunted growths peculiar to the summit. They heard no call of herder, no tinkle of bell, for the cattle that found summer pasturage here had been rounded up and driven home to the farms in the "flatwoods." The silence was intense; they saw no living creature save a buzzard circling high in the red skies of the sunset. Skimpy thought for a moment they were going down on the North Carolina side; he was about to protest; the way was indescribably rocky and tortuous; the night was coming on. Suddenly Binwell paused.

"Kem along, sonny; take the ladder in the middle an' feed it out ter me."

Skimpy, wondering, took the ladder in the middle, giving it a series of shoves toward Binwell, who suddenly lifted the end, and with one effort flung it from him — and out of the world, as it seemed to Skimpy.

He listened for a moment, hearing it crash among the tree-tops as it went falling down the precipice whence Binwell had thrown it. A moment after there was silence as intense as before. Then Binwell knelt on the verge and looked down the abyss. He raised a triumphant grinning face, and silently beckoned to Skimpy. The boy went forward and knelt too, to look over. At first he could see nothing but the shelving side of the mountain; the deep abyss gloomed with shadows, the richness of the autumnal colors sombre and tempered beneath the purple dusk. And then he discovered one end of the ladder, barely perceptible in the top of a pine-tree.

"It lodged 'mongst them pines," said the jubilant Binwell. "It's safe, summer or winter; nobody'll find it but the birds or the squir'ls."

Skimpy could no 'longer resist. "Air —

air — it yourn?" he faltered, struggling with his instinct of politeness.

Binwell had risen to his feet; he was rubbing the earth off his hands — recklessly bedaubed when he had knelt down — and also from his trousers, nimbly raising first one knee, then the other, for the purpose. He was chuckling unpleasantly as he looked at the boy.

"Ever see folks fling thar own ladders off'n the bluffs, an' land 'em 'mongst the tree-tops fur the birds ter roost in?"

Skimpy stared, and ruefully shook his head.

"Waal then! what ye talkin' 'bout?" Binwell's tone was cheerful, triumphant; a sinister triumph.

The dumfounded Skimpy faltered, —

"Whose war it, then?"

"Dunno edzac'ly," cried the blithe Binwell.

"Waal, now, that ain't fair!" protested Skimpy, indignantly. "I 'm goin' right down ter the Cove, and tell."

"Naw, ye won't! Naw, ye won't!" exclaimed the undismayed Binwell. "Ef ye do, ye'll git jailed quick 'n never war seen."

"I ain't done nothin'," cried Skimpy, recoiling.

"Ain't ye! Tote a man's ladder up the mounting, over ter the Carliny side, an' tumble it down 'mongst the pine tops, whar he'd hev ter make another ter reach it. Mebbe the constable an' old Greeps, ez be jestice o' the peace, don't 'low ez that's suthin', but I reckon they will!"

Skimpy was silent in acute dismay. Into what danger, what wrong-doing, had he not thrust himself by his disobedience! He looked at the grinning face, flushed by the fading remnant of the roseate sunset, feeling that he was in Binwell's power, wondering what he should do, how he should be liberated from the toils spread for him.

"See now, Skimp," said Binwell beguilingly, and the poor boy's heart leaped up at the kindly tone, for he sought to put the best construction on Jerry Binwell's intentions, if only to calm his own despair and distress. "I could jes' take ye under my arm — so," he tucked Skimpy's head under his arm and lightly lifted him high off his feet — " an' strong ez I be I could fling ye off'n that bluff half down that thar gorge; thar would n't be enough o' ye lef' ter pick up on a shovel; an' that would keep ye from tellin' tales on me, I reckon." He swung the boy perilously close to the edge of the precipice, then set him gently on his feet. " But I don't want ter hurt ye, an' I ain't goin' ter do it. I know ye air a plumb honer'ble, good sorter boy, an' ain't goin' ter make a tale-tell o' yerse'f, even if ye wouldn't git jailed. I wouldn't trest no boy I ever see but you-uns. I wouldn't trest Ike Guyther fur nuthin'. I war goin' ter tell you-uns all 'bout'n it ennyways, even 'fore I fund that thar ladder. An' then ye kin jedge whether I be right or wrong."

Skimpy, eager to be reassured, felt his heart lighten with the words. He strained his credulity to believe in Jerry Binwell. Surely he had not done so very wrong; there might be no harm in the man, after all. He drew a deep breath of relief, and then picked up his hat which had fallen from his head when Jerry Binwell was illustrating the terrible fate he might decree for the lad if he chose. The man was closely studying his face when their eyes met once more, but Binwell said simply that they had better go after Obadiah's fiddle or night would overtake them before they found it.

He talked as they went.

"Ye see, Skimpy," he said, "my tongue don't lay holt nat'rally ter the words, kase I hev got some things ter tell ez I ain't right proud on."

He glanced down at the wondering, upturned face, with its eyes wide with anticipation, and its mouth opening as if to swallow, without the customary grain of salt, any big tale which might be told.

"Ye hearn old Corbin say, yander at the store that day, ez I run durin' the War. An' I 'histed him up on the beam fur shamin' me 'fore all them folks. Waal, I ought n't ter done it, kase 't war true — *jes' one time!* I felt powerful 'shamed ter hear 'bout it ag'in — plumb bowed down."

The crafty eyes scanning Skimpy's ingenuous face saw that he was sympathetic.

"War ain't a healthy bizness, nohow," continued Jerry. "But thar air lots o' men, ez run heap more 'n me, ez don't hev it fetched up ag'in 'em every day. Lots o' runnin' war done in the War — but folks nowadays ginerally talks 'bout thar fightin'. Some nimble fellers showed their heels in them times — folks ez live right hyar in the Cove. But I be the only one ez hev got ter hear 'bout it in these days. It's kase I'm pore, Skimp. Ef I hed a good cabin an' right smart cornfield, an' consider'ble head o' stock, ye would n't hear 'bout my runnin' that time."

Cynicism is eminently infectious. Skimpy wagged his head significantly. "You would n't indeed!" the gesture seemed to say.

"They don't like me jes' kase I'm pore. An' kase I'm pore they call me shif'less. I hev hed a heap o' trouble; sech truck ez I hed I war obleeged ter spen' fur doctors' 'tendance on my wife, ez war ailin' always, an' arter all she died at last."

The unromantic Skimpy, meditating on the case, felt that at least the doctors' bills were at an end.

"An' now I be homeless, an' a wanderer, an' hev my leetle gal ter feed. Folks actually want ter take her away from me. Ef 't warn't fur her, them Guythers wouldn't let me stay thar a day."

Skimpy knew that this was true. Ike had confided so much to him of the family feeling on the matter.

"An' now folks in the Cove air a-fixin' ter drive me out'n it — me an' little Rosamondy. They can't set the law onto me, fur I never done nothin' ag'in it — so they be a-goin' ter laff me out'n it. Ye wanter know whose ladder that is?" he broke off with apparent irrelevance.

Skimpy nodded an eager assent.

"It's old Corbin's, I'll be bound, an' I'll tell ye why I 'low sech; no man but him kin do sech a job. Waal, ye know what he wants it fur? He wants somebody ez be light an' handy ter climb up Keedon Bluffs by it ter them hollows. An' ye wanter know what fur? Ter git suthin' ez air hid in one o' 'em. An' ye wanter know what that be?"

Skimpy's face in the closing dusk might have been cut out of stone, so white and set it was — such a petrified expectancy upon it. The man's eyes glittered as he held his own face nearer and spoke in a hissing whisper, albeit in the lonely wilderness none could hear his words.

"Some war maps, an' orders in a box what a courier — thinkin' he war a-goin' ter be captured — hid thar; an' he war killed afore ever he got 'em ag'in. An' long o' 'em air a letter a-tellin' 'bout me a-runnin' an' a-orderin' me ter be shot fur a deserter. An' old Corbin, bearin' a gredge ag'in me, air a-goin' ter perduce 'em an' fairly laff me out'n the Cove. An' I ain't got nowhar ter go."

"He's mighty mean!" cried Skimpy, his heart swelling with indignation.

"Waal, I wanter scotch his wheel!" exclaimed Binwell. "I don't want him ter do it."

"How kin ye purvent it?" said Skimpy, briskly. Surely there was no malice, no mischief on Binwell's part in this. His spirits had risen to their normal high pitch.

"Waal, Skimp, I hev been a-studyin' bout'n it. But till I fund that ladder — it air too long fur enny mortal place but Keedon Bluffs — an' made sure o' what he war a-doin' of, I war n't sati'fied in my mind. Ef ye'll holp me — kase I be too bulky nowadays ter creep in one o' them hollows — ef I'll kerry ye down thar will ye snake in an' git the box? Ye 'feared?"

For Skimpy had drawn back at this proposition. "Naw," he faltered, but with an affirmative tendency. He saw Binwell's teeth and eyes gleam through the dusk. This man *who ran* was laughing at him for being afraid of the great heights of Keedon Bluffs, of the black abysses below!

"We hed better hev tuk the ladder ter climb by," suggested Skimpy.

"An' hev old Corbin come along the river bank an' take it down whilst we war on it? I'm better'n enny ladder ye ever see, bein' so strong. Feel my arm," he held it out. "Shucks, boy! Fust time I ever see ye, ye war talkin' ter Ike 'bout climbin' down thar 'thout enny holp. But mebbe ef ye don't want ter go, Ike will. I hain't axed him yit. I'd ruther hev you-uns. But I reckon he ain't *afeard*."

In addition to Skimpy's sympathy for the ostracized Binwell his terror of being considered a coward was very great. "Naw — I'll go — I ain't 'feared; but I be powerful oneasy an' troubled bout'n that thar ladder."

"Waal, arter we git the box — the papers air in it — we'll go over to yon side o' the mounting with a axe, an' cut down the tree ez cotched the ladder, an' tote it back whar we fund it."

Skimpy's objections vanished at the prospect of being able to undo soon the harm he had done. He hoped fervently that old Corbin would not miss his ladder before it was replaced.

"Hyar's Obadiah's fiddle!" exclaimed Binwell, who led the way while the boy followed through the laurel, grown quite dark now; and when they emerged into the open woods they beheld the stars glistening in the shallows of the branch, and many a pensive glimmer came through the bare boughs, and through the thinning leaves.

XI.

THE ladder was early missed; indeed it was the next morning that old Corbin puffed and pushed through the laurel to the bare space where his handiwork had been wont to lie and to grow apace, rung by rung. He did not at first notice its absence. He put his box of tools on the ground. Then he sat down on a rock and mopped his brow with his red bandana handkerchief and gazed meditatively down the vistas of the woods. The Indian summer was abroad in the land, suffusing it with languor and light — a subtly tempered radiance; with embellishments of color, soft and brilliant; with fine illusions of purpling haze; with a pensive joy in sheer existence. How gracious it was to breathe such air, such aromatic perfumes; to hear such melodic sounds faintly piped with the wind among the boughs. Ah, summer, not going, surely! for despite the sere leaf one must believe it had barely come.

They were not poetic lungs which Mr. Corbin wore, encased in much fat, but they expanded to the exquisite aroma of the morning as amply as if they differentiated and definitely appreciated it. He drew several long luxurious sighs, and then it seemed as if he would breathe no more. He gasped; turned red; his eyes started from his head. He had taken notice at last that the ladder had been removed. He arose tremulously and approached the spot where it usually lay. There was no trace of it. He staggered a few steps backward in dismayed recoil. His spectacles fell to the ground, the lenses shattering on the stones.

"Witches!" he spluttered. "Witches!" He cast one terrified appealing look at the solitudes about him, half-fearing to see the mystic beings that his superstition deemed lurking there; then he began to waddle — for he could hardly be said to run — as fast as he could go along the path through the laurel.

Tremulous alike with his years and the shock of surprise, his condition was pitiable by the time he reached the store — for he at once sought his friend and crony the storekeeper. And some time elapsed before he could be restored to his normal calmness and make intelligible the detail of what had befallen him. Peter Sawyer was a man of considerable acumen. He was far more disposed to believe that the ladder had been found by some freakish boys who had mischievously hidden it in the laurel hard by, than that it had been spirited away by witches. He considered, however, that his old friend had been victimized beyond the limits of fun, and before setting out for the spot he summoned the constable of the district to their aid, for he felt that arrests for malicious mischief were in order. Both he and the officer were prepared to beat the laurel and patrol the neighborhood and ferret out the miscreants. They arranged their plans as they trudged on together, now and then pausing to wait for old Corbin as he pounded along behind them. The storekeeper was detailing, too, to the constable the reasons for the manufacture of the long ladder — for he was the confidential friend of Jake Corbin, and in fact had suggested the scheme.

"We mought ez well let ye inter the secret fus' ez las', kase this hyar case air one fur the strong arm o' the law." He threw back his narrow lizard-like head and laughed, showing his closely-set tobacco-stained teeth.

"Strong ez it air 't ain't plumb long enough!" he added.

The constable, a thick-set, slow man, cocked his head inquiringly askew.

"'T ain't long enough," continued Sawyer, enjoying the involutions of the method of disclosure he had adopted. "The arm o' the law ain't long enough ter reach up ter them hollows in Keedon Bluffs!"

"In Keedon Bluffs!" echoed the amazed officer.

"Jes' so," said Sawyer, laughing and nodding. "So we hev lengthened its reach by the loan of a ladder." He strode on silently for a few moments beside the constable, their two shadows following them down the red clay road, in advance of old Corbin, who was lumbering on behind attended by a portly, swaying, lunging image of himself, impudently magnified and nearly twice as big.

"Ye see," resumed Sawyer, "Jake Corbin b'lieves ez some o' old Squair Torbett's money an' sech, what he hid in the war times, air right up *yander* in one o' them holes — 't war this hyar Jerry Binwell, ez war a slim boy then, an' Ab Guyther ez holped ter hide it. Waal, ye know how things turned out. The Squair died 'fore many months were over an' them boys had run away to the Wars. Waal, ye know how cur'ous the heirs acted — looked sorter sideways when questioned, an' swore they never hed hed no money out'n Keedon Bluffs."

"I 'member," said the constable, "Ed declared out he never b'lieved thar war no money thar."

"Waal, Ed's dead, an' the tother heir moved ter Arkansas, an' the kentry-side ginerally b'lieved like them — that thar war n't no money thar — big fool tale. Waal, hyar kems back Jerry Binwell, arter twenty year, bein' pore ez Job's tur-r-key, an' takes ter a-loafin' roun' them Bluffs; I seen him thar twict myself. An' Ab Guyther hev tuk ter declarin' he wants ter climb down Keedon

Bluffs an' lay his hand on that thar old cannon-ball."

"Wants ter lay his hand on Squair's old money-box, ye better say," exclaimed Corbin.

"Waal now, I ain't goin' ter b'lieve nuthin' ag'in Ab!" exclaimed the constable excitedly.

"Ennyhow," wheezed old man Corbin, "we-uns 'lowed we'd git a ladder an' summons a officer an' take down that box, ef we could git a boy ter climb in, an' turn it over ter the law. Jerry Binwell ain't done nuthin' ez yit ter warrant arrestin' him, but we jes' 'lowed we-uns war n't a-goin ter set by an' let him put folks on beams an' steal money, an' loaf around ef thar war enny way ter pervent it."

The constable seemed to approve of the plan, and only muttered a stipulation that he did not believe Ab had anything to do with any rascality.

Little was said as they pushed through the tangle of the laurel. The storekeeper was ahead, leading the way, for he knew it well, having often come to consult his crony. "Waal, sir!" he exclaimed in indignant ruefulness when the bare rocky space was revealed along which the great ladder was wont to stretch. He glanced around excitedly at the constable, directing his attention to the spot, then called aloud, "Why, Jake," in a voice of exasperated compassion.

A cold chill was upon old Corbin as he waddled through the last of the tangled bushes; it required no slight nerve for him to again approach the place. He quivered from head to foot and wailed forth tumultuously, "I hev been snared by the witches. Le's git out'n these hyar witched woods! Don't ye reckon 't war the witches? It mus' hev been the witches!"

A new idea suddenly struck Peter Sawyer. "'T war n't no witches," he declared abruptly. "An' 't war n't no mischievous boys! 'T war Jerry Binwell; that's who hev got that ladder. Ef we-uns could ketch him a-nigh hyar I'd git him 'rested sure. He hev fund out what we air wantin' ter do."

"Better find the ladder an' git the box fust. We-uns don't want him — a rascal — ez much ez the law wants the Squair's money-box ter gin it back ter the heirs," said the cautious constable. "Go slow an' sure. Besides I don't wanter make no foolish arrests. The jestice would jes' discharge him on sech evidence ag'in him ez we kin show — kase we can't tell all we know, — fur the word would git all over the Cove, an' some limber-legged fellow mought climb up thar, an' ef he did n't break his neck he mought git the box. I tell ye — I'm a-goin' ter set a watch on them Bluffs from day-dawn till it's cleverly dark. An' ef that thar ladder be in these hyar woods I'll find it."

These wise counsels were heeded. Old Corbin started back to the store with his friend after one more apprehensive, tremulous, and searching glance for the witches' lair in the laurel which he dreaded to discover, and the constable took his way cautiously through the woods toward the river.

The morning wore on to the vertical noon-tide when the breeze died, and the shadows collapsed, and the slumberous purple haze could neither shift nor shimmer, but brooded motionless over the ravines and along the mountain slopes; the midday glowed, and burned with color more richly still, until the vermilion climax of the sunset made splendid the west, and tinged the east with gold and pink reflections. And all day the constable himself, hidden in a clump of crimson sour-wood, knelt on the summit of the Bluffs, watching the deep silent gliding of the river and the great sand-stone cliffs — with here a tuft of grass or a hardy bush in a niche, with sheer reaches and anon crevices, and on a ledge the ball from the deadly gun, lying silent and motionless in the sun.

Nothing came except a bird that perched on the cannon-ball; a mocking-bird, all newly plumed. He trimmed his jaunty wing, and turned his brilliant eye and his delicately poised head upward. Then, with his white wing-feathers catching the light, away he went to where the echoes awaited him. A star was in the river — its silver glitter striking through the roseate reflections of the clouds; and presently the darkness slipped down.

And the constable's joints were very stiff when he clambered out of the clump of sour-wood shoots.

XII.

It was a very dark night. The wind freshened; leaves were set adrift in the black void spaces; the jarring of bare boughs, continually clashing together, pervaded the gloom: the water was ruffled, and the reflection of the stars was distorted or annulled amongst the vacillating ripples as the faint beams fell. No other sound near Keedon Bluffs, no other stir.

By the fireside of Hiram Guyther's house one could hardly be unconscious of the tumult of the mountain forest, or of the swirl of the wind in the funnel-like depths of the Cove, however deep the reverie, however the fire might crackle as the big blazes sprang up the chimney, however the little Rosamondy might laugh or might sing.

"How the wind blows!" the blind man said from time to time, lifting his gray head and his young face. And aunt Jemima would remark on "the powerful clatter" of the orchard boughs and the rustling swish of the Indian corn standing dead and stark in the fields.

As the trumpeting blast came down the chimney once more Ab roused himself anew and exclaimed, "'Minds me o' the night Rosamondy kem."

"Did the wind blow me hyar?" cried Rosamondy, as she sat in her little chair.

"The bes' wind that ever blew!" declared aunt Jemima, her gleaming spectacles intercepting her caressing glance.

Jerry Binwell turned a trifle aside in his chair to hide the scornful curve of his lips. There was no need to shift his posture. Aunt Jemima's eyes were bent once more upon her knitting, and Abner was blind alike to sneers and smiles. Rosamond's attention was fixed upon a big red apple roasting and sputtering between two stones that served as fire-dogs. Now and then, with the aid of a stick, she turned the other side of the apple to the heat. Only the blinking cat saw the jeer on his face, and this animal was too frequently ridiculed to care to cultivate any fine distinctions in the nature of laughs. Curiously enough, the cat wore a queer gown of blue-checked homespun and a ruffled cap that was often awry, for she sometimes put up a disaffected paw to scrape it off, or it became disarranged in hasty or too energetic washings of her face. She had been thus accoutered by aunt Jemima to appease Rosamondy's craving for a live doll. The cat was very much alive, and seated before the fire she had an antique and dame-like look, which was highly appreciated by her owner, but which was totally destroyed when she walked on all-fours. The live doll was eminently satisfactory to Rosamond, and except for the tyranny of her garments was in danger of being killed by kindness.

The laugh on Jerry Binwell's face was only a transient gleam. He relapsed into brooding gravity and meditatively eyed the fire.

"Ab," he said suddenly, when aunt Jemima had left the room to join Mrs. Guyther, who was "sizin'" yarn in the shed-room, and he could hear their voices in animated controversy as to the best methods. "Ab,

I'll tell ye what this windy night in the fall of the year 'minds me of."

His voice had the most agreeable inflections of which it was capable, but it elicited no response, for Abner had not relented toward his old comrade, and seldom would seem aware of his existence. Binwell's face contorted into a disagreeable grimace. This secret taunt the blind man was spared. Then Binwell's smooth tones went on as if he had not expected a rejoinder.

"'Minds me o' that night in the old War time whenst me an' you-uns holped old Squair Torbett ter hide his plunder from g'rillas an' sech — ye 'member how the wind blowed?"

Abner's fire-lit face glowed with more than the reflection of the flames. His lip curled; the reminiscence seemed to afford him some occult amusement.

"I 'member! I 'member!" he said slowly; then he chuckled softly to himself.

Binwell's eyes were fixed upon him with an antagonistic intentness, as if he would fain seize upon his withheld thought in some unconscious betrayal of face. But the blind man could only hear his voice, languid and reminiscent, drawling on, aimlessly, it seemed. "Waal, I 'members it too, mighty well. How flustry the old man war! Wonder if we'll be that-a-way when we-uns git ez old ez him? He gin us the box, an' we-uns kerried it ter the top o' the Bluffs, an' ye clomb down whilst I watched. An' wunst in a while the old man would nudge me," then with a quick change of voice — "'Ain't that a horse a-lopin', Jerry? hear it? hear it?' An' I'd say, 'It's the wind, Squair — the wind, a-wallopin' up the gorge.' An' then he'd rest fur a minit an' say, 'Air sign o' Ab? That thar boy'll break his neck, I'm 'feared.' An' I'd say, 'I hear the clods in the niches a-fallin' whilst he climbs, Squair; he's a-goin' it.' An' then he'd clutch me by the arm, an' say, whispery an' husky, 'Jerry! Jerry! what's that down the road — the jingle o' spurs, the clank o' a sabre?' An' I'd say — 'It's jes' the dead leaves, Squair, a-rustlin' as they fly in the wind.' An' he war n't easy one minit till ye clomb up the Bluffs ag'in, empty-handed an' the box hid."

As he talked, Rosamond's hands had fallen still in her lap while she listened with the wide-eyed wonder of childhood. Her curling yellow hair, ruddily gleaming in the firelight, hung down over her shoulders, her cheek was flushed, her great gray eyes, full of starry lights and yet pensively shadowed by her long black lashes, were fixed upon his face. When the tension slackened she sighed deeply and stirred, and then lapsed into intent interest again.

The blind man had bent forward, his elbows on his knees. "I 'members," he said again.

"I never did know, Ab, whether ye fund them hollows in the Bluffs a toler'ble tight fit, nor how fur back they run in them rocks; but ye war a mighty slim boy in them days."

"War n't slim enough ter git inter the fust nor the second," spoke up the blind soldier briskly, with awakened interest.

"So ye put it inter the thurd?" demanded Jerry.

If he could have seen himself how well he would have thought it that his old comrade could not see him! His head was thrust forward till all the ligaments in his long thin neck were visible, strained and stretched. His eyes were starting. His breath was quick, and his under jaw had dropped. Rosamond had a half affrighted look as she sat in her chair on the hearth beside the sleeping dogs and the grotesquely attired cat that was gravely washing its face.

The blind man nodded. "Yes," he said simply, "I put it in the thurd, an' pritty far back, too."

The chimney was resounding with the burden of the blast as it sang without; its tumultuous staves echoed far up the mountain slopes. Abner lifted his head to listen, hearing perhaps the faint din of the winds of memory blowing as they listed about Keedon Bluffs. The next instant his attention was recalled. In the momentary absorption the sharpened hearing of the blind had failed him. He subtly knew that there was a change in the room, but what it was he could not say. He stretched out his hand with a groping gesture. "Jerry," he called out in a friendly voice. There was no answer.

The puzzled expression deepened on his face. He heard the stirring of the child. "Rosamondy," he said, "who's hyar?"

"Nobody," the vibrant, sweet voice answered, "nobody but me — an' Mis' Cat."

"Whar's Jerry?" he demanded.

"Gone out," she said promptly. "Sech walkin' on tiptoes I never see."

There sounded instantly a queer thumping on the puncheon floor, a tumble, a great gush of treble laughter; then the eccentric thumping was renewed and Abner knew that Rosamondy was imitating the deft celerity of Binwell's exit on tiptoes. He did not laugh. He leaned back in his chair with doubt and perplexity corrugating his brow.

A step was upon the ladder, descending from the roof-room — not Ike's usual light step, but he it was, slowly appearing from the shadows. Even after he had emerged into the genial firelight their gloom seemed still to rest upon his face, and his eyes were at once anxious and mournful. He withstood as well as he could the shock of welcome with which Rosamond rushed upon him, seizing him round the knees till he almost toppled over, and was constrained to wildly wave his arms in order to regain his equilibrium. She fell into ecstasies of delight because of the awkward insecurity he exhibited, and as with outstretched arms, and flying hair, and tangled feet, and rippling, gurgling cries, she mimicked him, he found himself at liberty to sink into a chair. And then while Rosamond, always long in exhausting her jokes, still toppled about the floor, he silently brooded over the fire.

Once or twice he raised his eyes and looked toward his uncle who seemed too lost in reverie. Sometimes Abner lifted his head to listen to the rioting winds and again bent it to his dreams. The white firelight flickered, and now the brown shadow wavered. He was presently subtly aware of a new presence by the hearth, unseen by others as all must be by him.

"Ye hev got trouble alongside o' ye, Ike," he remarked. "Ye're mighty foolish. It's a great thing ter be young, an' strong, an' hev all yer senses. The beastises hev got mo' gumption than ye. Ever see a young strong critter, free an' fat, that war mournful? Naw; an' ye ain't goin' ter. Ye hev got the worl' in a sling. An' ye set an' mope."

Ike made an effort to rouse himself. "I know I oughtn't," he said in a strained voice, "but I be mighty — mighty troubled."

"Jes' so," said the blind man.

Ike looked at the flickering white flames for a moment, at the pulsing red coals, at the vacillating brown shadows. Rosamondy had rushed into the shed-room to exhibit her imitation of Ike to his mother and aunt Jemima. He listened to the chorus of voices for a moment, then he said, "I dunno but what I'm foolish, uncle Ab, but I hearn what ye tole Jerry Binwell jes' now 'bout whar ye hid the Squair's money-box, an'— an' I wisht ye hedn't done it."

"What fur?" the blind man lifted his face lighted with sudden interest, "ye be 'feared ez he mought 'low it's thar yit an' go arter it an' git his neck bruk."

Ike moved uneasily.

"That's jes' the reason he tried to keep me

an' Skimpy Sawyer from climbin' down thar one evenin' — fust time I ever seen him; tried ter skeer we-uns with witches an' sech. The Squair's money-box air what he war arter, I be bound, the night o' the coon hunt whenst I cotch him thar. I'm feared he'll git it. I dunno what to do! I s'picioned suthin', but I never 'lowed 't war money. He'll git arrested ef he don't mind."

"I wisht he would," said Abner; he chuckled fiercely and fell to revolving his old grudges.

"Waal, I'd hate that mightily," said Ike dolorously, "arrested out'n we-uns's house. I war goin' ter tell dad nex' day, but he war gone 'fore I got home. I wisht Jerry Binwell hed never kem hyar!"

"Why, Ike," Abner retorted cogently, "then leetle Rosamondy would never hev kem!"

"I seen old Corbin an' the constable with thar heads mighty close tergether ter-day," Ike went on drearily, "an' arterward I passed down the river-bank on the opposite side ter Keedon Bluffs, an' I see the constable a-hidin' hisself in a clump o' sour-wood. I dunno what ter do. I feel 'sponsible, somehows. I don't want him ter git the money — a thievin' scamp — and yit I don't want him ter git arrested." He paused in astonishment.

Abner Guyther was laughing in sardonic delight. "He ain't goin' ter git the money!" he cried. "An' I dunno nobody ez needs arrestin' ez bad ez he do — somebody oughter scotch his wheel, sartain! G' long, Ike; g' long ter bed. An' quit addlin' yer brains 'bout'n yer elders."

Ike was not reassured by the reception of his disclosure. And he had not told the worst of his troubles. More than once of late he had seen Skimpy and Binwell together. He had felt no resentment that his friend had been forbidden association with him, to avoid contact with this elderly villain. It seemed wise in Skimpy's father, and he only wished that his own had been sufficiently uninfluenced and firm to have determined upon a similar course. Noting the constable in the clump of sour-wood, and with his own recollection of Binwell climbing down Keedon

Bluffs, he had been smitten with terror for Skimpy's sake. He knew that Binwell had some reason of his own for affecting the lad's society. In cudgeling his mind for the man's motive he had brought to light the true one which might not have been so readily presented were not Keedon Bluffs so continually in his thoughts of late. He was sure that Binwell wished Skimpy, being light and slim, to explore the hollows of the Bluffs — with what end in view he had not definitely known until to-night. Nevertheless the conviction that his simple-hearted friend had become involved in serious danger had been strong enough that afternoon to induce him to go to Skimpy's home. Old man Sawyer sat on the porch morosely smoking his pipe, and Ike paused at the fence and whistled for Skimpy — a shrill, preconcerted signal; it was in the deepest confidence that he was about to impart his suspicions and his warnings and he did not feel justified in including the elder Sawyer in the colloquy. It might be a slander on Jerry Binwell, after all. "An' I don't wanter be a backbiter like him," said Ike to himself.

The whistle brought Skimpy promptly out from the barn. To Ike's surprise, however, he did not approach the fence, which was at some distance from the house. He simply stood near the porch with his old hat on the back of his red head, his long arms crooked, his hands thrust into his pockets, and upon his face a sardonic grin that seemed broader than anything in his whole physical economy.

"Kem down hyar. I hev a word ter say ter ye," called Ike.

He felt as if he were dreaming when instead of replying Skimpy swayed himself grotesquely and mockingly about, and began to sing with outrageous fluctuations from the key "Oh - aw - e - Mister Coon ! Oh - aw - i - Mister Ky - une."

It seemed a frenzied imitation of himself, and Ike was about to speak when Skimpy, putting his fingers in his ears that he might not hear Ike, although to the casual observer it might well seem that he had good reasons for not wanting to hear himself, bellowed and piped mockingly, "Oh - aw - i - Mister Kyune! That's the way he 'lows I sing," he observed in an aside to his father, who might have been carved from a corn-cob, for all the animation he showed, except to silently smoke his corn-cob pipe.

"I never!" cried Ike indignantly; "somebody hev been settin' ye ag'in me — a back-bitin' scamp! An' I'll be bound I know who 't war."

But Skimpy's fingers were in his ears, and he was still swaying back and forth and making the air shudder with his mock vocalizations. At last Ike turned away in sheer futility, angered and smarting, but as anxious and troubled as before.

Now he was sorry he had not persisted for he had not realized how immediate and terrible was the danger to Skimpy. He sat still for a moment, afraid to say aught of the perplexities that racked him, lest being mistaken he might needlessly implicate Skimpy in any crime that Binwell might commit. Presently he rose with a look of determination on his face. The sound of the lifting latch, the cold in-rushing of the air, the light touch of the flakes of ashes set a-flying from the hearth, notified Abner that he was solitary by the fire. He heard the cat purring, the low murmuring of the flames in the chimney, the wind outside, the voices of the two women busy in the shed-room.

Another stir of a latch and a presence entered bright even to the blind man. "All alone-y by hisself-y!" Rosamondy cried as she pattered across the floor and flung herself into his arms. He shared much baby-talk with Mrs. Cat, but he was not jealous of that esteemed friend, for he was Rosamondy's preferred crony. Through her, life had come to mean for him a present as well as a past, and to hold for him a future and a vista. He planned for her with the two old women. He had let it be known to all his relatives that all he had in the world — his horse, his cows, his share of the cabin, his gun, a captured sabre — was to be hers at his death. Always in his simple dreams for enriching her, and for her fair fate, Jerry Binwell's image would be intruded like some ugly blight upon it all. He had heretofore thrust away the thought of him, and dreamed on resolutely. Somehow he could not do this to-night. As he patted her on the head and heard the silken rustle of her hair beneath his hand, he could but remember that it was her father risking his life on the rocks, his liberty, the lurking officer and everlasting ignominy, which must surely rebound upon her.

"She would n't know nuthin' 'bout it now, ef he war branded ez a thief, but she air a-goin' ter be a gal ez will keer mightily fur a good name an' sech. Jerry Binwell hain't never hed a good name wuth talkin' 'bout, but he ain't never yit been branded ez a thief."

Mrs. Cat was brought and perched upon his knee, and he was required to shake hands and inquire after her health and that of her family, which ceremony both he and the poor animal performed lugubriously enough, although with a certain dexterity, having been trained to it by frequent repetitions. Rosamondy, however, found herself a better improvisor than he of conversation for Mrs. Cat, and as she prattled on his anxious thoughts reverted to the subject.

"He air her dad, an' he 'll be disgraced fur

THE STORY OF KEEDON BLUFFS.

life, an' I could hev purvented it. Too late! Too late!" he groaned aloud.

He felt like a traitor as she passed her soft little arm around his neck and kissed his cheek — pale now, although it had never blanched for shot or shell. He had both her and Mrs. Cat to hold, and although both were of squirming tendencies his mind could still steadily pursue its troublous regrets.

"But I ought n't ter hev done it jes' fur Rosamondy, nuther. I oughter hev done it fur the sake of — *folks!* A man oughter keep another man from doing wrong, ef he kin, same ez ter keep his own score clear — them ez kin stan' ter thar guns oughter keer ter keep the whole line from waverin', stiddier a-pridin' tharse'fs on the aim o' thar one battery. Laws-a-massy; I wish I hed tole him. I wish I hed gin him a word. He mus' be nigh thar now. Ef I jes' could ketch him! Ef I jes' could find my way! I ain't been nigh thar fur twenty year. Fur one hour o' sight ter save a man from crime! Fur one hour o' sight to hold the battle-line! Fur one hour o' sight to do the Lord's kind will!"

He was speaking aloud. He had risen from his chair, the little girl and her cat slipping softly down upon the floor. He took a step forward, both groping hands outstretched. "Fur one hour o' sight!"

"I'll lead ye, unky Ab," the child compassionately exclaimed, putting up her soft, warm hand to his cold trembling fingers.

"Lead me! yes! Lead me ter Keedon Bluffs," he cried eagerly. "She kin do it! She kin save him! Stop," he caught himself. "Look out, Rosamondy. Air the night dark?"

She opened the door; a mild current of air flowed in above her yellow head, for the wind now was laid. She saw the dark woods gloom around; the stars glimmer in the vast spaces of the sky; but about the mountain summit shone an aureola of burnished gold.

"The moon's a-risin'," she said.

He placed his hand in hers; she stepped sturdily upon the ground. The door closed, and the hearth was vacant behind them but for the flicker of the flames, the drowsing dogs, and the purring Mrs. Cat.

XIII.

THAT night as Skimpy sat with the family group by the fireside in his father's cabin, he had much ado to maintain a fictitious flow of spirits, for at heart he was far from cheerful. Often he would pause, the laugh fading from his face, and he would lift his head as if listening intently. Surely the wind had no message for him as it came blaring down the mountain side! What significance could he detect in the clatter of the bare boughs of the tree by the door-step that he should turn pale at their slightest touch on the roof? Then recognizing the sound he would draw a deep breath of relief, and glance covertly about the circle to make sure that he had been unobserved. So expert in feigning had poor Skimpy become that he might have eluded all but the vigilance of a mother's eye.

"Air ye ailin', Skimpy?" she demanded anxiously. "Ye 'pear ter feel the wind. Ye shiver every time it blows brief. Be thar enny draught thar in the chinkin'?"

"Naw'm!" said Skimpy hastily. "I war jes' studyin' 'bout that thar song —

> "'The sperits o' the woods ride by on the blast,
> An' a witch they say lives up in the moon.
> Heigh! Ho! Jine in the chune!
> Jine in, neighbor, jine in the chune!'

"It jes' makes my marrer freeze in my bones ter sing that song," Skimpy said when his round fresh voice had quavered away into silence — somehow he could not sing to-night.

"Waal, I never set no store by sech," said his mother. She looked reassuringly at him over the head of the baby, who slept so much during the day that he kept late hours, and did his utmost to force the family to follow his example. He sat on her knee, sturdily upright, although she held her hand to his back under the mistaken impression that his youthful spine might be weak; but he had more backbone — literally and metaphorically — than many much bigger people. He was munching his whole fist, for his mouth seemed not only large but flexible, and as he gazed into the fire he soliloquized after an inarticulate fashion. His face was red; his head was bald except for a slight furze, which was very red, along the crown; notwithstanding his youth he looked both aged and crusty.

Bose was at his mistress's feet. He too sat upright, meditatively watching the fire with his one eye, and now and then lifting the remnants of his slit ears with redoubled attention as the wind took a fiercer twirl about the chimney. Occasionally as the baby's monologue grew loud and vivacious, Bose wagged the stump of his tail in joy and pride, and it thwacked up and down on the floor.

It was a very cheerful hearth — the grinding tidiness of Mrs. Sawyer showed its value when one glanced about the well-ordered room; at the clean pots and pans and yellow and blue ware on the shelves; at the bright tints of the quilts on the bed and of the hanks of yarn and strings of peppers hanging from the rafters that harbored no cobwebs; at the clear blazes unhindered by ashes.

Obadiah with his fiddle under his chin was

directly in front of the fire. He was tightening and twanging the strings; now and then cocking the instrument close to his ear to better distinguish the vibrations. There are few musicians who have a more capable and discerning air than Obadiah affected in those impressive moments of preparation. His three brothers sat on a bench, drawn across the hearth in the chimney corner, its equilibrium often endangered, for the two at one end now and again engaged in jocose scuffling, and Skimpy in the corner was barely heavy enough to keep it from upsetting. Sometimes their father, solemnly smoking his corn-cob pipe, would, with a sober sidelong glance and a deep half-articulate voice, admonish them to be quiet, and their efforts in this direction would last for a few moments at least. In one of these intervals their father spoke suddenly to Skimpy.

"I war downright glad ye tuk Ike up ez short ez ye done this evenin', Skimp," he said. "Though," he added, with an afterthought, "I don't want ye to gin yerse'f up ter makin' game o' folks."

"'T war him ez fust made game o' me," said Skimpy, ruefully, the taunt devised by the ingenious Binwell still rankling deep in his simple heart.

The twanging fiddle-strings were suddenly silent. Obadiah looked up with a fiery glance. "What gin the critter the insurance ter make game o' you-uns, Skimp?" he demanded angrily.

Until today Skimpy had never mentioned his grievance, so deeply cut down was his self-esteem, and so reduced his pride in his "gift in quirin'." He had hardly understood it himself, but he dreaded to have the family know how low his powers were rated lest they too think poorly of them. For Skimpy himself had come to doubt his gift — the insidious jeer had roused the first self-distrust that had ever gnawed him. His voice no longer sounded to him so full, so sweet, and loud, and buoyant. He sang only to quaver away, forlorn and incredulous after the first few tones. No more soaring melodies for him. He could only fitfully chirp by the wayside.

"He 'lowed," said Skimpy, turning red,

"ez I couldn't sing — ez Bose, thar, could sing better'n *me* — hed a better voice; Bose, yander, mind ye."

Bose at the sound of his name looked up with a sleepy inquiry in his single eye. Skimpy did not notice, but began to wheeze and rasp forth, —

"'Oh-aw-ee-ye, Mister Kyune, Oh, Mister Kyune!' That's the way he 'lowed I sing."

"Dell-law!" Obadiah's flexible lips distended in a wide and comprehensive sneer that displayed many large irregular teeth, and was in more ways than one far from beautiful. But to Skimpy no expression had ever seemed so benignant, indicating as it did the strength of fraternal partisanship.

"He's jes' gredgin' ye, Skimp," cried Obadiah. "Else he be turned a bodacious idjit! He air a idjit fur the lack o' sense! Shucks!" — his manner was the triumph of lofty contempt as he again lifted his violin to his ear — "don't ye 'sturb me ag'in 'bout Ike Guyther. Don't ye, now."

The two boys who sat at the end of the bench talked together, so eager were they to express their scorn. "The whole Smoky Mountings knows better'n that!" cried one belligerently.

"Nobody kin sing like Skimpy—sings like a plumb red-headed mocking-bird, an' Ike knows that fac' ez well ez road ter mill," said the other.

His mother had almost dropped the baby, who made a great lunge toward Bose. "Why," she cried, "Skimpy gits his singin' ways right straight from his gran-dad Grisham — *my* dad — ez war knowed ter be the mos' servigrous singer they hed ennywhar roun' in this kentry fifty year ago. I hev hearn all the old folks tell 'bout'n his singin' an' his fiddlin' when he war young, an' I 'members he sung fune'l chunes whenst he war a old man; he hed gin up the ways o' the worl' an' he wouldn't sing none 'ceptin' 'round the buryin' groun' whenst they war c'mittin' some old friend ter the yearth. An' his voice would sound strange — strange, an' sweet an' wild, like the water on the rocks in a lonesome place, or the voice of a sperit out'n the sky. Oh my! — oh my!" — she was rocking herself to and fro with the baby in her arms, her distended eyes looking far down the vistas of the past. "How I 'members it — how I 'members it!"

Hark! Skimpy starts with a sudden shock. Was that the beating of the boughs on the roof, drum-like, or a rub-a-dub measure played with two pea-sticks on the rail fence of the garden — the signal by which Jerry Binwell was to summon him should he conclude to try the hazardous enterprise this night? The wind — only the wind; wild weather without! Thankful he was to be left to this cheerful fireside, and the warm partisan hearts so near akin to him.

"I wonder ye didn't larrup Ike, Skimpy," said Obadiah. "Ye could do it. He's heavy, but mighty clumsy. Ye could run aroun' him fifty times whilst he war a-turnin' his fat sides roun'."

Obadiah knitted his brows and nodded confidently at Skimpy.

"I never thunk 'bout fightin'," responded Skimpy. "My feelin's war jes' so scrabbled up I never keered fur nuthin' else! Arter Ike an' me hed been so frien'ly too!"

"That's like my dad. Skimpy's like his gran-dad," said Mrs. Sawyer, dreamily. "He war tender an' easy hurt in his feelin's."

Like that saintly old man! How *could* she think it. Skimpy was ready to burst into tears. And yet, he argued, there was nothing wicked about what he was to do. He wished only to help Jerry Binwell to secure the box of papers that could do naught but harm now — to help a man who could have no other aid. Why did the enterprise terrify him as a crime might? he asked himself in exasperation. Certainly as far as he could see there was no mischief in it. As far as he could see! Alas, Skimpy! How shortsighted a boy is apt to be! He began to say to himself that it was because everybody was down on Binwell, being poor and therefore unpopular, that he too was influenced by the prevalent feelings, even when he sought to be friendly. Yet this reasoning was specious. If it had involved no disobedience, his heart would have been light enough. He could have gone along gayly with his father, whom he trusted, and explored every chasm and cavity in Keedon Bluffs, or, for the matter of that, in the Great Smoky Mountains. But as he listened for the summons — a faint travesty of a drum-beat on the rail fence — he would grow rigid and pale, and when the boughs swaying in the blast touched with quick, tremulous twigs the clapboards of the roof with a tapping sound, he shivered, and started from his seat, and fell back again, hot and cold by turns.

"I be glad fur ye ter hev no mo' ter do with them Guythers, ennyhow," said his father gravely. "They hev acted mighty strange bout'n Jerry Binwell — an' ef they consorts with sech ez him me an' mine can't keep in sech comp'ny. Folks hev tuk ter specla'tin' powerful bout'n Ab an' him hevin' been sech enemies — Ab war blinded through his treachery — an' now livin' peaceable together under one roof. Some folks 'low ez Ab hev got his reasons fur it, an' they ain't honest ones. I ain't a-goin' ter pernounce on that; I ain't a-goin ter jedge, kase I don't want ter be jedged. I reckon I'd show up powerful small — though honest — thar ain't no two ways 'bout that, I thank the mercy. But ye done mighty well, Skimpy, ter gin up yer frien' like I tole yer ter do thout no questions, kase this Binwell war thar. Ye 'll l'arn one day ez I hed a reason — a mighty good one, too."

He sucked his pipe sibilantly. "Ye done mighty well, Skimpy," he repeated with an earnest sidelong glance at his son.

Skimpy listened, half choking with the confession that crowded to his lips. And yet how could he divulge that he had given up Ike indeed for Binwell himself; how could he confide Binwell's secret of the Bluffs, the story of the courier and his hidden box and the order to be shot as a deserter; and above all, how could he admit having assisted in throwing away old Corbin's ladder — the malice and the mischief of it frightened him even yet.

"I 'll tell ez soon ez I kin put it back. I 'll tell dad ennyhows; I hev got ter holp Jerry Binwell this time, but arter that I 'll never go along o' him ag'in," he thought, as he stared pale and abstractedly at his father, who was tilted back in his chair contentedly smoking his pipe.

Obadiah twanged gleefully on his fiddle while the firelight and shadows danced to the measure; the other two boys scuffled merrily with one another, sometimes leaving the bench to "wrastle" about the floor, falling heavily from time to time. The baby sputtered and crowed and grabbed Bose's ear in a strong mottled fist until that amiable animal showed the white of his eye in gazing pleadingly upward at the infantile tyrant. The wind whirled about the house, the door shook, and the branches of the tree close by thrashed the roof.

"Why, Skimpy, how mournful ye look!" exclaimed Mrs. Sawyer.

"Shucks!" said Obadiah fraternally, "ye need n't be mournin' over Ike an' his comp'ny. I would n't gin a pig-tail, nor a twist of one, fur Ike!"

"Ye hev got comp'ny a plenty at home," exclaimed Mrs. Sawyer, "with yer three big brothers"—

"An' the baby," cried one of the wrestlers pausing for breath.

"An' Bose," added the other, red-faced and panting.

"Laws-a-massy, Skimp," exclaimed Obadiah, rising to the heights of heroism, "I'll gin ye the loan o' my fiddle. Thar!"

He placed the instrument in Skimpy's trembling hand, and laid the bow across his knee. And this from Obadiah, who had always seemed without feeling except for his own music!

Their kindness melted Skimpy, who held the instrument up to his agitated face as if to shield it from observation, and burst into tears.

"Waal, sir!" exclaimed the wrestlers in chorus.

"Tut — tut — Skimpy boy!" said his father in remonstrance.

Obadiah's face was anxious. "Jes' lean a leetle furder ter the right, Skimp," he said, "don't drap no tears inter the insides o' that thar fiddle — might sp'ile it tee-totally."

Skimpy held the violin well to one side, and wept as harmlessly as he might. He found a great relief in his sobs, a relaxation of the nervous tension — he might have told them all then had it not been for the inopportune solicitude of his mother.

"Ye hed better go ter bed, sonny. I know it's early yit, but ye look sorter raveled out. Ye better go ter bed an' git a good sleep, an' ye won't keer nuthin' 'bout Ike an' his aggervations in the mornin'."

Skimpy, still carefully holding the precious violin, sat on the bench for a moment longer, struggling with that extreme reluctance to retire which is characteristic of callow humanity. But he felt that it would be better to be out of the sight of them all; he might be tempted to say or do something that he would regret afterward; he rose slowly, and with an averted face, held the fiddle and bow out toward Obadiah who grasped them with alacrity, glad enough that his generosity had not resulted in the total destruction of the instrument in which his heart was bound up. Skimpy with slow tread and a downcast look which greatly impressed the two sympathetic wrestlers, who were standing still now and gravely gazing after him, took his way up the ladder in the corner which ascended into the roof-room of the cabin. He paused when he had almost reached the top, turned and glanced down doubtfully at the group below.

The flames, yellow and red, filled all the chimney, and the little room was brave in the golden glow. Already the two wrestlers were again matching strength in friendly rivalry, seizing each other by the waist, and swaying hither and thither with sudden jerks to compass a downfall — their combined shadow on the wall reeling after them seemed some big, frightful two-headed monster. Obadiah's cheek was tenderly bent upon the violin; a broad smile was on his face as the whisking bow in his deft handling drew out the tones. The baby's stalwart grip on Bose's ear had begun to elicit a long, lingering, wheezing whine for mercy, not unlike the violin's utterance; it ended in a squeak before Mrs. Sawyer noticed how the youngster was enjoying himself.

"Pore Bose!" she cried as she unloosed the mottled pink and purple fist, and then with a twirl she whisked the baby around on her lap with his back to his victim. A forgiving creature was Bose, for as the baby's bald head turned slowly on its neck and the staring round eyes looked after the dog, Skimpy could hear his stump of a tail wagging in cheerful fealty to the infant, and thwacking the floor — although the wrestlers were unusually noisy, although the violin droned and droned, and although the winds sang wildly without and the sibilant leaves whirled.

Skimpy hesitated even then for a moment as he stood on the ladder; finally he mounted the remaining rungs, his story untold.

It was not very dark in the roof-room; through the aperture in the floor, where the ladder came up, rose the light from the fire below, and there were many cracks which served the same purpose of illumination. Skimpy could see well enough the two beds where he and his brothers were wont to sleep. Garments hung from the rafters, familiar some of them and often worn, and others were antique and belonged to elders in the family long ago dead; these had never been taken down since placed there by their owners; several were falling to pieces, shred by shred, others were still fresh and filled out, and bore a familiar air of humanity.

Skimpy did not approach the beds, he quietly crossed the room to the gable end, paused to listen, then opened the batten shutter of a little glassless window beside the chimney. Dark — how dark it was as he thrust out his head; he started to hear a dull swaying of the garments, among the rafters, as if they clothed again life and motion. Only the illusion of the wind, he remembered, as he strove to calm the tumultuous throbbing of his heart, his head instinctively turning toward the fluttering vestments that he could barely see.

The wind still piped — not so sonorous a note, however; failing cadences it had and dying falls, as of a song that is sung to the end. Once again the boughs beat upon the eaves — and, what was that! Skimpy's heart gave a great plunge, and he felt the blood rush to his head. A faint clatter — a ra-ta-ta, beaten drum-like on the rail fence of the "garden spot" — or was it his fancy?

The wind comes again down the gorge.

The althea bushes and the holly shiver together. The dead Indian corn, standing writhen and bent in the fields, sighs and sighs for the sere season. And the boughs of the tree lash the roof. An interval. And once more — ra-ta-ta! from the garden fence! And ra-ta-ta, again.

XIV.

THE group below took no heed how the time passed. Thinking of it afterward, they said it seemed only a few moments before they heard amongst the fitful gusts of the wind, wearing away now, and the dull stirring of the tree without, a hurried, irregular footstep suddenly falling on the porch, a groping, nervous hand fumbling at the latch.

"Hev ye los' yer manners ez ye can't knock at the door," said Peter Sawyer sardonically, speaking through his teeth, for he still held his pipe-stem in his mouth.

Ike had burst in without ceremony and stood upon the threshold, holding the door in one hand and gazing about with wild eyes, half blinded by the light, uncertain whether Skimpy was really absent or overlooked among the rest.

"I — I — kem ter see Skimpy," he faltered.

Mrs. Sawyer had set the baby on the floor beside Bose, and had folded her arms stiffly. She looked at Ike with heightened color and a flashing eye.

"Waal, I ain't keerin' ef ye never see Skimpy ag'in," she said indignantly, "considerin' the way ye treat him. That thar boy air tender in his feelin's, an' he hev been settin' hyar an' cryin' his eyes out 'count o' you-uns. Ye want ter torment him some mo', I s'pose."

Ike stared bewildered. "I ain't never tormented Skimp none ez I knows on."

"Ye ain't!" exclaimed Obadiah, scornfully. Then grotesquely distorting his face he careened to one side and began to wheeze distractingly — "Oh — aw — yi-i, Mister Ky-une, Oh — aw — ee-ee, Mister Ky-une."

As Ike still stood holding the door open, the flames bowed fantastically before the wind, sending puffs of smoke into the room and scurrying ashes about the hearth.

"Kem in, ef ye air a-comin', an' go out ef ye air a-goin'," said Mrs. Sawyer tartly. "Ennyhow we-uns will feel obligated ef ye'll shet that door."

The invitation was none too cordial, but Ike availed himself of the opportunity to speak, since the matter was so important.

He closed the door and sat down on the end of the bench where Skimpy had been sitting so short a time before.

"Skimp 'lows that's the way ye mocked him," said Obadiah. "An' ye wants ter see him ag'in, do ye? Ef I war Skimp I'd gin ye sech a dressin' ez ye wouldn't want ter see *me* ag'in soon." He winked fiercely at Ike and nodded his head. Then he stuck his violin under his chin and began to saw away once more as if nothing had happened.

Ike gave a great gulp as if he literally swallowed a bitter dose in taking Obadiah's defiance; the strain on his temper was severe, but he succeeded in controlling himself. It was in a calm and convincing voice that he said : —

"Oby, ye an' me, an' Skimp, and the t' others" — pointing to the tangled-up wrestlers — "hev been too good frien's ter be parted by folks tattlin' lies an' tales from one ter 'nother. I never said sech. I never mocked

Skimpy's singin' sence I been born. I hev sot too much store by Skimp fur that, an' he oughter know it."

Mrs. Sawyer's expression softened. "Ye only would hev proved yerse'f a idjit ef ye hed faulted Skimpy's singin'," she said. Then, still more genially — "Set up closer ter the fire. It mus' be airish out'n doors. Who d' ye reckon tole Skimp sech a wicked, mean story on ye?"

Ike trembled in his eagerness to tell. "I dunno fur true, Mis' Sawyer, and mebbe I ought n't ter say, but I b'lieves it be Jerry Binwell, kase Skimpy hev been goin' a powerful deal with him lately, an'" —

Peter Sawyer turned suddenly upon the boy. "The truth ain't in ye, Ike Guyther. Ye knows ez yer dad an' yer uncle, an' yerse'f an' yer folks ginerally, air the only critters in the Cove ez would 'sociate with Jerry Binwell, an' live in fellowship with him under the same roof. I 'low they air crazy — plumb bereft. It's yer folks ez hev harbored him hyar, an' ye can't tar Skimpy with sayin' he consorts with sech. I forbid Skimp ever ter go with you-uns enny mo', so 's ter keep him out'n Binwell's way. Now, sir; ye can't shoulder him off on Skimpy!"

Ike's face turned scarlet. "I hev glimpsed Skimp with him ag'in an' ag'in. An' I b'lieves he be a-goin' ter git Skimp inter mischief."

Obadiah laid his fiddle down on his knee, pursed up his lips, and looked aggravatingly cross-eyed at Ike, up from his toes to the crown of his head.

"'T would n't take much mo', Ike, ter make *me* settle you-uns," he observed.

"I ain't keerin' fur you-uns, Obadiah!" cried Ike. "I hev kem ter say my say — an' I'm a-goin' ter do it. I b'lieve Jerry Binwell air arter old Squair Torbett's money what folks 'low he hid in a box in a hollow o' Keedon Bluffs."

Peter Sawyer's pipe had fallen from his hand, and the fire and tobacco and ashes rolled out upon the hearth. He gave it no heed. He sat motionless, leaning forward, his elbows on his knees, his surprised, intent eyes fixed upon the boy's face.

"I never s'picioned at fust what he war arter, though I seen him foolin' roun' them Bluffs an' a-climbin' on the ledges. But I knowed 't war suthin' cur'us. An' whenst I seen Skimp along o' him so much I kem hyar this evenin' an' tried ter warn him. But ter-night I hearn Jerry Binwell ax uncle Ab — him it war ez holped the Squair hide the box whilst Jerry Binwell watched — what hollow he hid it in."

"An'—an'—did Ab tell him?" demanded Peter Sawyer, leaning down, his excited face close to Ike's, his eyes full of curiosity and more — intention, suspicion.

Once again Ike recognized the false position into which his uncle was thrust. How could any man's honest repute survive a misunderstanding like this? He realized that in his eager desire to save his friend his tongue had outstripped his prudence.

"I jes' wanter tell Skimp what I hearn," he said, declining to answer categorically, "an' then let him go on with Binwell ef he wants ter. I war feared he'd purvail on Skimp, by foolin' him somehows, ter snake inter them hollows an' git that box fur him. Whar be Skimp?"

"Asleep in bed, whar he oughter be, Ike," said Skimpy's mother contentedly rocking by the fire.

Peter Sawyer hesitated for a moment. Then he slowly rose. "'T won't hurt Skimp ter wake him up. He mought ez well hear this ez not."

He winked at his wife. He thought that if Skimpy were present he himself would hear more of the whereabouts of the box, which might prove of service in the constable's search for it, when the ladder could be found or a substitute provided. He walked toward the primitive stairway, feeling very clever and a trifle surprised at the promptitude and acumen of his decision. He himself would wake Skimpy in order to give him a quiet caution not to become involved in any quarrel that might restrain or prevent Ike's disclosure. He tramped slowly and heavily up the ladder as if he were not used to it, and indeed he seldom ascended into the roof-room, its chief use being that of a dormitory for the boys. As he left the bright scene below, suffused with mellow light, the shadows began to gloom about him as if they came down a rung or two to meet him or to lend him a helping hand; he raised his eyebrows and peered curiously about. His head was hardly above the level of the floor of the loft before he became aware that the roof-room was full of motion. He gave a sudden start, and stood still to stare, to collect his senses that surely had played him false. No, — solemnly wavering to and fro, a pace here, a measure there, was the gaunt company of old clothes, visible in the glimmer through the crevices of the floor, and bearing the semblance of life in the illusions of the faint light and the failing shadow, as if they had outwitted fate somehow, despite their owners' mounds in the little mountain graveyard. Peter Sawyer gasped — then he shivered. And it was, perhaps, this involuntary expression of physical discomfort which led his mind to judge of cause and effect. "The winder mus' be open," he said through his chattering teeth.

The next moment he saw it — he saw the

purplish square amidst the darkness of the walls; the naked boughs of the tree without; and high, high — for he was looking upward — the massive looming mountain, and the moon, the yellow waning moon, rising through the gap in the range.

"The wind's laid," he muttered, "or the flappin' o' that thar shutter would hev woke the boy afore this time."

He clumsily ascended the remaining rungs and strode across the floor to Skimpy's bed, looking now with curious half-averted eyes at the lifelike figures of the old clothes, and then at the yellow moon shining through the little window into the dusky place, and drawing the shadow of the neighboring tree upon the floor.

Sawyer's hand touched the pillow.

"Skimpy!" he said. And again, "Skimpy!"

It was a louder tone. A penetrating quality it had, charged as it was with a sudden, keen fear.

"Fetch a light!" he cried, running to the top of the ladder, dashing away the spectral garments. "Fetch the lantern, Oby, or a tallow dip."

Below they heard his quick footsteps returning to the bed as they sprang up, affrighted, yet hardly knowing what had happened.

"Skimpy!" his voice sounded strong again — reassured; he could not, would not believe this thing. "Quit foolin', sonny; whar hev ye hid?"

Skimpy's mother had waited for neither the candle nor the lantern; she mounted the ladder by the light of the fire, and she understood what had happened almost as soon as Ike did, as pale and dismayed he looked over her shoulder into the dusky garret. The golden moonlight fell through the little window upon the slowly-pacing clothes, and drew the image of the bare tree upon the floor, and slanted upon the empty bed by which Peter Sawyer stood crying aloud — "He hev gone, wife; he hev gone!"

XV.

The great gray sandstone heights of Keedon Bluffs began to glimmer in the midst of the black night when the yellow moon, slow and pensive, showed its waning disk, half veiled with a fibrous mist, in the gap of the eastern mountain. The woods were still densely dark on the other side of the road. A slender beech, white and spectral, was dimly suggested at their verge, shuddering and shivering in the last vagrant gust of the wind. Skimpy glanced fearfully at it for a moment as he came softly down the road and then he stood shivering too, with his hands in his pockets.

A swift, dark figure, as noiseless as if unhampered with substance, appeared at his side, and a husky, wheezing voice murmured suddenly — "Hyar we air, Skimp!"

Even so bated a tone did not elude the alert echo. "S-Skimp-imp-mp," the Bluffs were sibilantly multiplying the tones. It seemed to Skimpy that some vague spy of the earth or of the air was repeating the sound to charge its memory with the word. He could ill trust even Keedon Bluffs with the secret of his name now, and he looked with futile deprecation over his shoulder at every whisper of the familiar word.

"Don't talk!" he said nervously.

"Shucks!" exclaimed Binwell; "I'd sing ef I war minded ter — an' ef I hed a pipe like yourn. What ails ye ter be so trembly? 'Tain't no s'prisin' job — it's fun, boy! An' ter-morrer ye and me will go an' cut down them pines an' git old Fat-sides' ladder out'n 'em."

Skimpy plucked up a little. The prospect of retrieving his folly reassured him. It was the hour, the secrecy of his escape from the roof-room window at home, the atmosphere of mystery that surrounded the adventure, he endeavored to think, rather than any distrust of Jerry Binwell, which shook his nerves. He lent himself with docile acquiescence to a sort of harness of rope which the man slipped over his head and secured beneath his armpits, one end fastened to Binwell's arm. Its ostensible use was to aid the boy while climbing, in case he should slip among the ledges. A mind prone to suspicion might have deemed its utility most pronounced in preventing Skimpy from hiding anew or making off with anything of value which he might find hidden in the hollows.

There were no shadows on the brow of the precipice when the golden rays from the moon rested broadly upon the road or journeyed in long stately files down the sylvan vistas. Both man and boy had slipped from the verge, and were clambering along the jagged, oblique ledges of the Bluffs, Skimpy often stayed and helped by the strong hand of the other. The moon was higher now in the sky. A white radiant presence suddenly began to walk upon the water. Down between the banks it came, upon the lustrous darkness of the current and the mirrored shadows, diffusing softest splendor, most benignant and serene. Skimpy, pausing to rest, hearing the stir of the pines on the opposite bank and the musical monotone of the river, stood mopping his brow and clinging to the strong arm held out to him; he abruptly pointed out the reflection of the moon to his companion, and asked if it did not remind him of that night on a distant sea when Christ came walking along the troubled waves.

A sudden great lurch! It was not Skimpy, but Binwell — the athlete — who started abruptly, and almost fell from the Bluff into the water far below. He recovered himself with an oath.

"Ain't ye got no better sense, ye weasel! 'n ter set out with sech senseless, onexpected gabble in sech a job ez this? Naw, it don't look like nuthin' — nuthin' but a powerful onlucky wanin' moon, a-showin' how the time's a-wastin'. Ye hustle yer bones else I'll drap ye down thar an' then ye'll find out what's walked on the water."

Skimpy said nothing; he heartily wished he was on the top of Keedon Bluffs once more. Their steps dislodged now and then a bit of stone from the rock that fell with a ringing sound against the face of the Bluffs into the river. Sometimes clods dropped with a muffled thud; every moment the moon grew brighter. There were no more stoppages on the way. Binwell urged the boy on whenever he would pause for breath, and it was not long before they were near the gaping cavities that looked grewsome and uninviting enough as Skimpy approached. He cast one despairing glance up at the face of the cliffs — it seemed that he could never again stand on the summit, so long, so toilsome was the way. He might have thought it short enough with some hearty comrade. For Binwell's grasp was savage now on the boy's arm; he cursed Skimpy under his breath whenever a step faltered. He no longer cared to be smooth, to propitiate. "He'd take me by the scruff o' the neck, an' pitch me into the ruver ef I did n't do his bid now, bein' ez I can't holp myself," thought Skimpy, appalled.

A pity that a boy cannot inherit his father's experience — but must learn wisdom as it were under the lash!

Very black indeed the first of the cavities was as he passed; he hardly dared look within the embrasure-like place; no grim muzzle of a gun he beheld, no bursting shell flung forth; only a bat's soft, noiseless wings striking him in the face as he climbed by on the ledge below. The second hollow was passed too, and now for the third. Binwell stopped the boy, and began to rearrange the cords beneath his arms. "Confound ye," he said, his fingers trembling over the knots as he lifted his eyes reproachfully to the boy's face, "ye hev got me plumb upset with yer fool talk — I 'lowed jes' now I hearn leetle Rosamondy a-callin' me."

The rocks were vibrating softly — but could the echoes of Keedon Bluffs repeat the fancy of a sound!

Skimpy stretched his arm into the cavity as far as it might go, half expecting it to be snatched by the claw of a witch; but no — his empty palm closed only on the clammy air.

"Up with ye!" said Jerry impatiently.

One moment — and there were the duskily purple mountains, the gray obscurity of the misty intervals, the lustrous darkness of the river, the fair sky, and the reigning moon; then the vault-like blackness of the hollow.

The boy scuffled along it for a few moments, "snakin' it," he called the process, and feeling like so much pith in the bark. Binwell still paid out the cord as Skimpy crept further and further, and then —

What was the matter with the rocks! Endowed with Rosamond's voice they called him again and again, with dulcet treble iteration that was like the fine vibrations of a stringed instrument all in tune. He listened, paling a little; it was no fancy; he was discovered. He stood his ground for the nonce. What affinity for harm and wrong! The coward might be brave for a space.

Another voice; he jerked nervously at the cord on Skimpy's arm. It was Abner's voice; he was on the summit of the Bluffs. He too was calling aloud:

"Kem up, Jerry, 't ain't no use. Kem up."

Jerry made no answer; he muttered only to himself, "Ye 'll fall off'n the aidge o' that Bluff unbeknown ter yerse'f, ole mole!"

Abner began anew and all the echoes were pleading and insistent. "Kem up, Jerry! Ye'll be deesgraced fur life, and hyar's leetle Rosamondy a-waitin' fur ye!"

Jerry was standing breathless, for Skimpy within was suddenly motionless. Then the cord grew slack in his hand, for the boy was coming out backward.

Binwell gave no heed to the commotion on the summit. A heavy, clanking metallic sound had caught his ear — it was the money-box of the Squire which the boy was dragging out, every moment coming nearer to that clutching, quivering hand.

Ah, Rosamond, calling in vain! Give it up, old soldier! No battle-cry of honor can rally comrades like this. But they pressed perilously close to the edge of the cliff — the blind man and the little child — beginning to sob together with dreary helplessness and futility, and casting their hopeless entreaties upon the night air, the echoes joining their pleas with wild insistence, and the forest silence holding its breath that no wistful word might be lost.

And thus others found them, shadowy figures as stealthily approaching as if the blind man could see, and the confiding little child wonder; — two, three, four, five figures pausing on the summit of the cliff, watching in intensest excitement the man on the ledge, and, slowly emerging from the cavity, dragging after him an iron box twelve inches square perhaps and weighty to handle, a boy, slight, agile, unmistakable.

Skimpy, covered with dust, choking, out of breath, confused by the sound of voices on the summit and the clamor of the echoes, hardly knew how it was that he should hear in the medley the familiar tones of his father calling on Heaven to pity him, for his son was a thief! He heard too the voice of the child and the blind soldier's entreaties. And then the sharp tones of the constable rang out — "Surrender thar — or I fire!" His senses reeled as Binwell, catching the box from his hands, turned and with quick leaps like a fox's clambered on down the ledges. The cord was still about Skimpy's shoulders; with a sharp twist he came to his knees in great pain; then the end of the rope swung slack below, and he knew that Binwell had just cut it to liberate himself — a great splash in the river told that he had taken to the water and the constable's bullet whizzed by the Bluffs a second too late.

"He'll hev ter gin up the box time I light out arter him," cried the constable; "I'll meet up with him by the ruver-bank. He can't run fur with a heavy box full o' gold an' silver."

There was no use in keeping the secret longer.

"It's full o' sand!" cried the blind man with dreary contempt in the fact. "The Squair kerried it full o' sand whenst he buried it — jes' fur a blind. He knowed Jerry s'picioned he hed money an' he never trested him. Jerry kep' watch, an' I clomb the Bluffs, an' hid the box. Whar the Squair an' me actially hid the money war in a hollow o' one o' the logs o' his house, an' thar's whar the money war kep' till the e-end o' the war. The heirs knowed it all the time. Write ter Arkansas an' ax the one ez be livin' thar."

A relish was added to the excitement which the events produced throughout the Cove next day by the gossips' speculations on Binwell's disappointment — how he must have looked, what he must have said, when he felt sufficiently safe to open the box and found it full of sand. For he made good his escape, the pursuit being given over instantly upon the discovery that he had stolen nothing worth having. The constable contented himself with declaring that he should never again come within the district save to be ushered into the county jail. The neighborhood cronies congregated at the store and talked the matter over, each having some instance of Binwell's duplicity to relate. All were willing enough to credit Peter Sawyer's account of how Skimpy had been deluded into assisting Binwell's scheme by the pretense that there were only papers hidden in the box which he had a right to destroy. Notwithstanding the fact that no suspicion rested upon him, Skimpy was not for a long time so blithe a lad as before he climbed down Keedon Bluffs. And he is ready now to believe that his father learned a good many things in those years of seniority which are still unknown to him, and he has some respect for experience. It is not necessary to scald him now in order to convince him that boiling water is — as it is said to be — hot.

The blind man's story was amply confirmed by a letter from the surviving heir who had been told by his father of the hoax of the hidden box, and who had always relished its mystery, since it had served its purpose and had diverted plunder and search from the hoard concealed in the wall.

At Hiram Guyther's cabin, however, the gossip had no zest. For the first time a deep gloom had fallen on the blind soldier's face as he sat in his enforced inactivity, a-wasting his life away in the chimney corner. His gray hair hardly seemed so incongruous now, for an ashen furrowed pallid anxiety had replaced the florid tints of cheek and brow. Sometimes he would rise from his chair and stride back and forth the length of the room; now and again a deep sigh would burst from him.

"I would n't mind it, Ab," Mrs. Guyther

would say in her comforting soft drawl. "Ye done all ye could — more 'n enny other man would, 'flicted with blindness. Fairly makes me shiver whenst I 'member ye an' Rosamondy walkin' along them cliffs in the dead o' night like ye done."

"She'll never be able ter live through it when she finds out 'bout her dad; she's a gal ez be a-goin' ter hev a heap o' feelin's," he would groan, with prescient grief for the gay Rosamond's future woes. "It'll plumb kill her ter know she don't kem o' honest folks. Ef it don't — it's wuss yit; fur it'll break her sperit, an' that's like livin' along 'thout a soul; sorter like walkin' in yer sleep."

And even Ike's mother could say naught to this.

Only on aunt Jemima's countenance a grim satisfaction began to dawn. She was not an optimist; nevertheless she contrived to extract a drop of honey from all this wormwood.

"It's all fur the bes' — I've hearn that preached all my days. Ev'y body knowed ennyhow ez he war mean enough fur ennything — ter steal, ef 'casion riz. An' he war her dad; could n't git roun' that! All's fur the bes'! Ef he hed hev stayed he mought hev tuk a notion ter kerry Rosamondy away from hyar. *Now* he don't dare ter show his nose hyar ag'in. An' we hev got Rosamondy safe an' sure fur good an' all."

So she knitted on with a stern endorsement of the course of events expressed in her firmly-set lips and the decisive click of her needles.

Even this view did not mitigate Abner's grief, and he sorrowed on for Rosamondy's sake.

The secret of Keedon Bluffs once discovered was spread far and wide. The news, crossing the ranges, penetrated other coves, and was talked of round many a stranger's hearth. Even to Persimmon Cove, where Jerry Binwell had married, the story came, albeit tardily. It was told first there by the sheriff, who had chanced to be called to that remote and secluded spot in pursuit of some evil doer hiding in the mountains, and he gave to the constable, as he passed through Tanglefoot

Cove on his way to the county town, sundry items, gathered during his stay in Persimmon Cove, which that functionary felt it was his duty to communicate to the Guythers.

It was a widow whom Jerry Binwell had married in Persimmon Cove — a young woman with one child; and when he left the place after her death, he took his stepdaughter with him; some people said his motive was to spite her grandmother, with whom he had quarreled, and who had sought to claim her; others said that it was because the little Rosamond contrived to keep a strong hold on the heart of every creature that came near her, and had even won upon Jerry Binwell. Certain it was that old Mrs. Peters, her grandmother, had heard with great delight the tidings of Rosamond's whereabouts, and the sheriff had promised her to acquaint with the facts the family with whom the child lived.

Every member of the household felt stunned as by a blow when the constable had left them to their meditations. Even Rosamond, with all her merry arts, could not win a smile from the grave and troubled faces grouped about the fire, and she desisted at last; she leaned her head, with its floating lengths of golden hair, against the brown logs of the wall, and looked wistfully at them all with a contemplative finger in her pink mouth.

"She hev ter go!" said the upright Hiram Guyther with a sigh, "she ain't ourn ter keep."

"We hev ter gin her up," groaned the blind man.

Mrs. Guyther looked wistfully at her with moist eyes, and dropped a half-dozen stitches in her knitting.

And aunt Jemima suddenly threw her blue-checked cotton apron over her head, and burst into a tumult of passionate tears. "I wisht," she exclaimed — wicked old soul! — "thar warn't no sech thing ez right an' wrong! But I don't keer fur right. An' I don't keer fur wrong. They shan't take my child away from hyar."

Although it wrung their hearts they decided to relinquish their household treasure. But they temporized as well as their scanty tact would enable them. A message was sent to old Mrs. Peters, coupled with an invitation to come and make them a visit. And thus they eked out the weeks.

One day — a day of doom it seemed to them — there rode up to the door a small wizened old woman, sharp-eyed, with a high voice and a keen tongue; she was riding a white mare with a colt at her heels. She scarcely seemed perturbed by Rosamond's reluctance to recognize her. The alert eyes took in first with an amazed stare the child's cleanly and whole attire, her delicately tended flowing hair, her fine, full, glowing look of health; then with more furtive glances she expended what capacity for astonishment remained to her on the scoured puncheon floor, the neat women and men, the loom, with a great roll of woven cloth of many yards hanging to it; the evidences of a carefully adjusted domestic routine, of thrift and decorum and moral worth; the cooking and quality of the meal presently set forth on the table. She had not lived so long in this world to be unable to recognize sterling people when she met them.

They all talked on indifferent topics for a time. But presently she broke forth.

"I dunno ez I oughter up an' remark it so flat-footed — but I never expected ter find Jerry Binwell's friends sech ez you-uns. I would n't hev rid my mare's back sore ef I hed. I dunno ez I 'd hev kem at all."

"Waal," said Hiram Guyther, "I reckon 't war leetle Rosamondy ez jes' tangled herself up in our heart-strings — an' that made us put up with Jerry. We 'lowed he war her dad."

"I 'm powerful glad he ain't!" said Abner.

"I say!" cried the sharp little woman scornfully. "*Her dad* war a mighty solid, 'sponsible, 'spectable young man, an' good-lookin' till you could n't rest!" He 'd hev lived till he war eighty ef his gun hed n't bust an' killed him. I dunno what ailed Em'line ter marry sech ez Jerry arterward. He made way with everything her fust husband lef' her, an' mighty nigh all I hed, 'mongst his evil frien's an' drinkin'. But he always war mighty good ter Rosamondy. I 'll gin him that credit."

"Ennybody would be good ter sech a child ez Rosamondy!" cried aunt Jemima.

"Waal, we war all frien's ter Jerry, ez fur ez he'd let us be, an' ter the leetle gal," said Hiram, solidly, "an' I hope, mum, ye'll let her spen' cornsider'ble of her time with us."

This was the cautious way it began, although it fired aunt Jemima's blood to hear the permission humbly craved instead of claimed as a right.

But Mrs. Peters smilingly accorded it. She herself had entered upon a long visit; whenever she made a motion to return, the family so vehemently demurred that she relented, only stipulating that when she should depart aunt Jemima should accompany her. She took a sad pleasure in the talk of the blind artillery-man, her own son, who was killed in battle, having been in the same command. Abner remembered him after a time, and told her many things of his army life which she had not before known. She had a sort of maternal tenderness for his comrade, and loved to see how Rosamond had blossomed in the waste places of his life.

"I don't think 't would be right ter take her away from Ab," she said, when the visit was at last at an end. And so only the two old women went to Persimmon Cove; together they came back after a time. And thus for years, the old cronies, cherishing so strong a bond of friendship, have vibrated on visits to and fro. But whoever comes or goes Rosamond has never yet left the hearthstone made brighter by her presence.

And when she and the blind artillery-man walk hand in hand down the shady road to Keedon Bluffs, she always cries out gleefully when she sees the great cannon-ball arrested midway on the ledge, and he tells her again how it must have burst forth from the muzzle of the gun far away, and, sounding its shrill battle cry, whirled through the air, describing a great arc against the sky, dropping at last, spent and futile, on the ledge there above the river.

"Sometimes," he says, "sometimes, Rosamondy, I feels ez ef I 'd like ter lay my hand on that ball ef I could git nigh it — 'minds me so o' the war times; 't would bring 'em nigher; they seems a-slippin' away now."

"I hate that cannon-ball; it kem so nigh a-killin' somebody," says Rosamondy, "an' I hate war times. An' I don't want folks ter be hurted no mo'."

And in the deep peace of the silent mountain fastnesses and the sheltered depths of the Cove, they leave the old ball, spent and mute and harmless, lying on the ledges of Keedon Bluffs, above the reddening river, and take their way homeward through the sunset glow.

Standard and Popular Library Books

SELECTED FROM THE CATALOGUE OF

HOUGHTON, MIFFLIN AND COMPANY.

A Club of One. An Anonymous Volume, $1.25.

Brooks Adams. The Emancipation of Massachusetts, crown 8vo, $1.50.

John Adams and Abigail Adams. Familiar Letters of, during the Revolution, 12mo, $2.00.

Oscar Fay Adams. Handbook of English Authors, 16mo, 75 cents; Handbook of American Authors, 16mo, 75 cents.

Louis Agassiz. Methods of Study in Natural History, Illustrated, 12mo, $1.50; Geological Sketches, Series I. and II., 12mo, each, $1.50; A Journey in Brazil, Illustrated, 12mo, $2.50; Life and Letters, edited by his wife, 2 vols. 12mo, $4.00; Life and Works, 6 vols. $10.00.

Anne A. Agge and Mary M. Brooks. Marblehead Sketches. 4to, $3.00.

Elizabeth Akers. The Silver Bridge and other Poems, 16mo, $1.25.

Thomas Bailey Aldrich. Story of a Bad Boy, Illustrated, 12mo, $1.50; Marjorie Daw and Other People, 12mo, $1.50; Prudence Palfrey, 12mo, $1.50; The Queen of Sheba, 12mo, $1.50; The Stillwater Tragedy, 12mo, $1.50; Poems, *Household Edition*, Illustrated, 12mo, $1.75; full gilt, $2.25; The above six vols. 12mo, uniform, $9.00; From Ponkapog to Pesth, 16mo, $1.25; Poems, Complete, Illustrated, 8vo, $3.50; Mercedes, and Later Lyrics, cr. 8vo, $1.25.

Rev. A. V. G. Allen. Continuity of Christian Thought, 12mo, $2.00.

American Commonwealths. Per volume, 16mo, $1.25.
   Virginia. By John Esten Cooke.
   Oregon. By William Barrows.
   Maryland. By Wm. Hand Browne.
   Kentucky. By N. S. Shaler.
   Michigan. By Hon. T. M. Cooley.

Kansas. By Leverett W. Spring.
California. By Josiah Royce.
New York. By Ellis H. Roberts. 2 vols.
Connecticut. By Alexander Johnston.

(In Preparation.)

Tennessee. By James Phelan.
Pennsylvania. By Hon. Wayne MacVeagh.
Missouri. By Lucien Carr.
Ohio. By Rufus King.
New Jersey. By Austin Scott.

American Men of Letters. Per vol., with Portrait, 16mo, $1.25.

Washington Irving. By Charles Dudley Warner.
Noah Webster. By Horace E. Scudder.
Henry D. Thoreau. By Frank B. Sanborn.
George Ripley. By O. B. Frothingham.
J. Fenimore Cooper. By Prof. T. R. Lounsbury.
Margaret Fuller Ossoli. By T. W. Higginson.
Ralph Waldo Emerson. By Oliver Wendell Holmes.
Edgar Allan Poe. By George E. Woodberry.
Nathaniel Parker Willis. By H. A. Beers.

(In Preparation.)

Benjamin Franklin. By John Bach McMaster.
Nathaniel Hawthorne. By James Russell Lowell.
William Cullen Bryant. By John Bigelow.
Bayard Taylor. By J. R. G. Hassard.
William Gilmore Simms. By George W. Cable.

American Statesmen. Per vol., 16mo, $1.25.

John Quincy Adams. By John T. Morse, Jr.
Alexander Hamilton. By Henry Cabot Lodge.
John C. Calhoun. By Dr. H. von Holst.
Andrew Jackson. By Prof. W. G. Sumner.
John Randolph. By Henry Adams.
James Monroe. By Pres. D. C. Gilman.
Thomas Jefferson. By John T. Morse, Jr.
Daniel Webster. By Henry Cabot Lodge.
Albert Gallatin. By John Austin Stevens.
James Madison. By Sydney Howard Gay.
John Adams. By John T. Morse, Jr.

John Marshall. By Allan B. Magruder.
Samuel Adams. By J. K. Hosmer.
Thomas H. Benton. By Theodore Roosevelt.
Henry Clay. By Hon. Carl Schurz. 2 vols.
(*In Preparation.*)
Martin Van Buren. By Edward M. Shepard.
George Washington. By Henry Cabot Lodge. 2 vols.
Patrick Henry. By Moses Coit Tyler.

Martha Babcock Amory. Life of Copley, 8vo, $3.00.

Hans Christian Andersen. Complete Works, 10 vols. 12mo, each $1.00. New Edition, 10 vols. 12mo, $10.00.

Francis, Lord Bacon. Works, 15 vols. cr. 8vo, $33.75; *Popular Edition*, with Portraits, 2 vols. cr. 8vo, $5.00; Promus of Formularies and Elegancies, 8vo, $5.00; Life and Times of Bacon, 2 vols. cr. 8vo, $5.00.

L. H. Bailey, Jr. Talks Afield, Illustrated, 16mo, $1.00.

M. M. Ballou. Due West, cr. 8vo, $1.50; Due South, $1.50.

Henry A. Beers. The Thankless Muse. Poems. 16mo, $1.25.

E. D. R. Bianciardi. At Home in Italy, 16mo, $1.25.

William Henry Bishop. The House of a Merchant Prince, a Novel, 12mo, $1.50; Detmold, a Novel, 18mo, $1.25; Choy Susan and other Stories, 16mo, $1.25; The Golden Justice, 16mo, $1.25.

Bjornstjerne Bjornson. Complete Works. New Edition, 3 vols. 12mo, the set, $4.50; Synnove Solbakken, Bridal March, Captain Mansana, Magnhild, 16mo, each $1.00.

Anne C. Lynch Botta. Handbook of Universal Literature, New Edition, 12mo, $2.00.

British Poets. *Riverside Edition*, cr. 8vo, each $1.50; the set, 68 vols. $100.00.

John Brown, A. B. John Bunyan. Illustrated. 8vo, $4.50.

John Brown, M. D. Spare Hours, 3 vols. 16mo, each $1.50.

Robert Browning. Poems and Dramas, etc., 15 vols. 16mo, $22.00; Works, 8 vols. cr. 8vo, $13.00; Ferishtah's Fancies, cr. 8vo, $1.00; Jocoseria, 16mo, $1.00; cr. 8vo, $1.00; Parleyings with Certain People of Importance in their Day, 16mo or cr. 8vo, $1.25. Works, *New Edition*, 6 vols. cr. 8vo. $10.00.

William Cullen Bryant. Translation of Homer, The Iliad

cr. 8vo, $2.50; 2 vols. royal 8vo, $9.00; cr. 8vo, $4.00. The Odyssey, cr. 8vo, $2.50; 2 vols. royal 8vo, $9.00; cr. 8vo, $4.00.

Sara C. Bull. Life of Ole Bull. *Popular Edition.* 12mo, $1.50.

John Burroughs. Works, 7 vols. 16mo, each $1.50.

Thomas Carlyle. Essays, with Portrait and Index, 4 vols. 12mo, $7.50; *Popular Edition*, 2 vols. 12mo, $3.50.

Alice and Phœbe Cary. Poems, *Household Edition*, Illustrated, 12mo, $1.75; cr. 8vo, full gilt, $2.25; *Library Edition*, including Memorial by Mary Clemmer, Portraits and 24 Illustrations, 8vo, $3.50.

Wm. Ellery Channing. Selections from His Note-Books, $1.00.

Francis J. Child (Editor). English and Scottish Popular Ballads. Eight Parts. (Parts I.–IV. now ready). 4to, each $5.00. Poems of Religious Sorrow, Comfort, Counsel, and Aspiration. 16mo, $1.25.

Lydia Maria Child. Looking Toward Sunset, 12mo, $2.50; Letters, with Biography by Whittier, 16mo, $1.50.

James Freeman Clarke. Ten Great Religions, Parts I. and II., 12mo, each $2.00; Common Sense in Religion, 12mo, $2.00; Memorial and Biographical Sketches, 12mo, $2.00.

John Esten Cooke. My Lady Pokahontas, 16mo, $1.25.

James Fenimore Cooper. Works, new *Household Edition*, Illustrated, 32 vols. 16mo, each $1.00; the set, $32.00; *Fireside Edition*, Illustrated, 16 vols. 12mo, $20.00.

Susan Fenimore Cooper. Rural Hours. 16mo, $1.25.

Charles Egbert Craddock. In the Tennessee Mountains, 16mo, $1.25; Down the Ravine, Illustrated, $1.00; The Prophet of the Great Smoky Mountains, 16mo, $1.25; In The Clouds, 16mo, $1.25.

C. P. Cranch. Ariel and Caliban. 16mo, $1.25; The Æneid of Virgil. Translated by Cranch. 8vo, $2.50.

T. F. Crane. Italian Popular Tales, 8vo, $2.50.

F. Marion Crawford. To Leeward, 16mo, $1.25; A Roman Singer, 16mo, $1.25; An American Politician, 16mo, $1.25.

M. Creighton. The Papacy during the Reformation, 4 vols. 8vo, $17.50.

Richard H. Dana. To Cuba and Back, 16mo, $1.25; Two Years Before the Mast, 12mo, $1.00.

G. W. and Emma De Long. Voyage of the Jeannette. 2 vols. 8vo, $7.50; New One-Volume Edition, 8vo, $4.50.
Thomas De Quincey. Works, 12 vols. 12mo, each $1.50; the set, $18.00.
Madame De Stael. Germany, 12mo, $2.50.
Charles Dickens. Works, *Illustrated Library Edition*, with Dickens Dictionary, 30 vols. 12mo, each $1.50; the set, $45.00.
J. Lewis Diman. The Theistic Argument, etc., cr. 8vo, $2.00; Orations and Essays, cr. 8vo, $2.50.
Theodore A. Dodge. Patroclus and Penelope, Illustrated, 8vo, $3.00. The Same. Outline Illustrations. Cr. 8vo, $1.25.
E. P. Dole. Talks about Law. Cr. 8vo, $2.00; sheep, $2.50.
Eight Studies of the Lord's Day. 12mo, $1.50.
George Eliot. The Spanish Gypsy, a Poem, 16mo, $1.00.
Ralph Waldo Emerson. Works, *Riverside Edition*, 11 vols. each $1.75; the set, $19.25; *"Little Classic" Edition*, 11 vols. 18mo, each, $1.50; Parnassus, *Household Edition*, 12mo, $1.75; *Library Edition*, 8vo, $4.00; Poems, *Household Edition*, Portrait, 12mo, $1.75; Memoir, by J. Elliot Cabot, 2 vols. $3.50.
English Dramatists. Vols. 1–3, Marlowe's Works; Vols. 4–11, Middleton's Works; Vols. 12–14, Marston's Works; each vol. $3.00; *Large-Paper Edition*, each vol. $4.00.
Edgar Fawcett. A Hopeless Case, 18mo, $1.25; A Gentleman of Leisure, 18mo, $1.00; An Ambitious Woman, 12mo, $1.50.
Fénelon. Adventures of Telemachus, 12mo, $2.25.
James T. Fields. Yesterdays with Authors, 12mo, $2.00; 8vo, Illustrated, $3.00; Underbrush, 18mo, $1.25; Ballads and other Verses, 16mo, $1.00; The Family Library of British Poetry, royal 8vo, $5.00; Memoirs and Correspondence, cr. 8vo, $2.00.
John Fiske. Myths and Mythmakers, 12mo, $2.00; Outlines of Cosmic Philosophy, 2 vols. 8vo, $6.00; The Unseen World, and other Essays, 12mo, $2.00; Excursions of an Evolutionist, 12mo, $2.00; The Destiny of Man, 16mo, $1.00; The Idea of God, 16mo, $1.00; Darwinism, and Other Essays, New Edition, enlarged, 12mo, $2.00.
Edward Fitzgerald. Works. 2 vols. 8vo, $10.00.
O. B. Frothingham. Life of W. H. Channing. Cr. 8vo, $2.00.
William H. Furness. Verses, 16mo, vellum, $1.25.

Gentleman's Magazine Library. 14 vols. 8vo, each $2.50; Roxburgh, $3.50; *Large-Paper Edition*, $6.00. I. Manners and Customs. II. Dialect, Proverbs, and Word-Lore. III. Popular Superstitions and Traditions. IV. English Traditions and Foreign Customs. V., VI. Archæology. VII. Romano-British Remains: Part I. (*Last two styles sold only in sets.*)

John F. Genung. Tennyson's In Memoriam, cr. 8vo, $1.25.

Johann Wolfgang von Goethe. Faust, Part First, Translated by C. T. Brooks, 16mo, $1.25; Faust, Translated by Bayard Taylor, cr. 8vo, $2.50; 2 vols. royal 8vo, $9.00; 2 vols. 12mo, $4.00; Correspondence with a Child, 12mo, $1.50; Wilhelm Meister, Translated by Carlyle, 2 vols. 12mo, $3.00. Life, by Lewes, together with the above five 12mo vols., the set, $9.00.

Oliver Goldsmith. The Vicar of Wakefield, 32mo, $1.00.

Charles George Gordon. Diaries and Letters, 8vo, $2.00.

George H. Gordon. Brook Farm to Cedar Mountain, 1861-2. 8vo, $3.00. Campaign of Army of Virginia, 1862. 8vo, $4.00. A War Diary, 1863-5. 8vo, $3.00.

George Zabriskie Gray. The Children's Crusade, 12mo, $1.50; Husband and Wife, 16mo, $1.00.

F. W. Gunsaulus. The Transfiguration of Christ. 16mo, $1.25.

Anna Davis Hallowell. James and Lucretia Mott, $2.00.

R. P. Hallowell. Quaker Invasion of Massachusetts, revised, $1.25. The Pioneer Quakers, 16mo, $1.00.

Arthur Sherburne Hardy. But Yet a Woman, 16mo, $1.25; The Wind of Destiny, 16mo, $1.25.

Bret Harte. Works, 6 vols. cr. 8vo, each $2.00; Poems, *Household Edition*, Illustrated, 12mo, $1.75; cr. 8vo, full gilt, $2.25; *Red-Line Edition*, small 4to, $2.50; *Cabinet Edition*, $1.00; In the Carquinez Woods, 18mo, $1.00; Flip, and Found at Blazing Star, 18mo, $1.00; On the Frontier, 18mo, $1.00; By Shore and Sedge, 18mo, $1.00; Maruja, 18mo, $1.00; Snow-Bound at Eagle's, 18mo, $1.00; The Queen of the Pirate Isle, Illustrated, small 4to, $1.50; A Millionaire, etc., 18mo, $1.00; The Crusade of the Excelsior, 16mo, $1.25.

Nathaniel Hawthorne. Works, "*Little Classic*" *Edition*, Illustrated, 25 vols. 18mo, each $1.00; the set $25.00; *New Riverside Edition*, Introductions by G. P. Lathrop, 11 Etchings and Portrait, 12 vols. cr. 8vo, each $2.00; *Wayside Edition*, with Introductions, Etchings, etc., 24 vols. 12mo, $36.00;

Fireside Edition, 6 vols. 12mo, $10.00; The Scarlet Letter, 12mo, $1.00.

John Hay. Pike County Ballads, 12mo, $1.50; Castilian Days, 16mo, $2.00.

Caroline Hazard. Memoir of J. L. Diman. Cr. 8vo, $2.00.

Franklin H. Head. Shakespeare's Insomnia. 16mo, parchment paper, 75 cents.

The Heart of the Weed. Anonymous Poems. 16mo, parchment paper, $1.00.

S. E. Herrick. Some Heretics of Yesterday. Cr. 8vo, $1.50.

George S. Hillard. Six Months in Italy. 12mo, $2.00.

Oliver Wendell Holmes. Poems, *Household Edition*, Illustrated, 12mo, $1.75; cr. 8vo, full gilt, $2.25; *Illustrated Library Edition*, 8vo, $3.50; *Handy-Volume Edition*, 2 vols. 32mo, $2.50; The Autocrat of the Breakfast-Table, cr. 8vo, $2.00; *Handy-Volume Edition*, 32mo, $1.25; The Professor at the Breakfast-Table, cr. 8vo, $2.00; The Poet at the Breakfast-Table, cr. 8vo, $2.00; Elsie Venner, cr. 8vo, $2.00; The Guardian Angel, cr. 8vo, $2.00; Medical Essays, cr. 8vo, $2.00; Pages from an Old Volume of Life, cr. 8vo, $2.00; John Lothrop Motley, A Memoir, 16mo, $1.50; Illustrated Poems, 8vo, $4.00; A Mortal Antipathy, cr. 8vo, $1.50; The Last Leaf, Illustrated, 4to, $10.00.

Nathaniel Holmes. The Authorship of Shakespeare. New Edition. 2 vols. $4.00.

Blanche Willis Howard. One Summer, Illustrated, 12mo, $1.25; One Year Abroad, 18mo, $1.25.

William D. Howells. Venetian Life, 12mo, $1.50; Italian Journeys, 12mo, $1.50; Their Wedding Journey, Illustrated, 12mo, $1.50; 18mo, $1.25; Suburban Sketches, Illustrated, 12mo, $1.50; A Chance Acquaintance, Illustrated, 12mo, $1.50; 18mo, $1.25; A Foregone Conclusion, 12mo, $1.50; The Lady of the Aroostook, 12mo, $1.50; The Undiscovered Country, 12mo, $1.50.

Thomas Hughes. Tom Brown's School-Days at Rugby, 16mo, $1.00; Tom Brown at Oxford, 16mo, $1.25; The Manliness of Christ, 16mo, $1.00; paper, 25 cents.

William Morris Hunt. Talks on Art, 2 Series, each $1.00.

Henry James. A Passionate Pilgrim and other Tales, 12mo, $2.00; Transatlantic Sketches, 12mo, $2.00; Roderick Hudson, 12mo, $2.00; The American, 12mo, $2.00; Watch and Ward, 18mo, $1.25; The Europeans, 12mo, $1.50; Confidence, 12mo, $1.50; The Portrait of a Lady, 12mo, $2.00.

Anna Jameson. Writings upon Art Subjects. New Edition, 10 vols. 16mo, the set, $12.50.

Sarah Orne Jewett. Deephaven, 18mo, $1.25; Old Friends and New, 18mo, $1.25; Country By-Ways, 18mo, $1.25; Play-Days, Stories for Children, square 16mo, $1.50; The Mate of the Daylight, 18mo, $1.25; A Country Doctor, 16mo, $1.25; A Marsh Island, 16mo, $1.25; A White Heron, 18mo, $1.25.

Rossiter Johnson. Little Classics, 18 vols. 18mo, each $1.00; the set, $18.00.

Samuel Johnson. Oriental Religions: India, 8vo, $5.00; China, 8vo, $5.00; Persia, 8vo, $5.00; Lectures, Essays, and Sermons, cr. 8vo, $1.75.

Charles C. Jones, Jr. History of Georgia, 2 vols. 8vo, $10.00.

Malcolm Kerr. The Far Interior. 2 vols. 8vo, $9.00.

Omar Khayyám. Rubáiyát, *Red-Line Edition*, square 16mo., $1.00; the same, with 56 Illustrations by Vedder, folio, $25.00; The Same, *Phototype Edition*, 4to, $12.50.

T. Starr King. Christianity and Humanity, with Portrait, 12mo, $1.50; Substance and Show, 16mo, $2.00.

Charles and Mary Lamb. Tales from Shakespeare. *Handy-Volume Edition.* 32mo, $1.00.

Henry Lansdell. Russian Central Asia. 2 vols. $10.00.

Lucy Larcom. Poems, 16mo, $1.25; An Idyl of Work, 16mo, $1.25; Wild Roses of Cape Ann and other Poems, 16mo, $1.25; Breathings of the Better Life, 18mo, $1.25; Poems, *Household Edition*, Illustrated, 12mo, $1.75; full gilt, $2.25; Beckonings for Every Day, 16mo, $1.00.

George Parsons Lathrop. A Study of Hawthorne, 18mo, $1.25.

Henry C. Lea. Sacerdotal Celibacy, 8vo, $4.50.

Sophia and Harriet Lee. Canterbury Tales. New Edition. 3 vols. 12mo, $3.75.

Charles G. Leland. The Gypsies, cr. 8vo, $2.00; Algonquin Legends of New England, cr. 8vo, $2.00.

George Henry Lewes. The Story of Goethe's Life, Portrait, 12mo, $1.50; Problems of Life and Mind, 5 vols. 8vo, $14.00.
A. Parlett Lloyd. The Law of Divorce, cloth, $2.00; sheep, $2.50.
J. G. Lockhart. Life of Sir W. Scott, 3 vols. 12mo, $4.50.
Henry Cabot Lodge. Studies in History, cr. 8vo, $1.50.
Henry Wadsworth Longfellow. Complete Poetical and Prose Works, *Riverside Edition*, 11 vols. cr. 8vo, $16.50; Poetical Works, *Riverside Edition*, 6 vols. cr. 8vo, $9.00; *Cambridge Edition*, 4 vols. 12mo, $7.00; Poems, *Octavo Edition*, Portrait and 300 Illustrations, $7.50; *Household Edition*, Illustrated, 12mo, $1.75; cr. 8vo, full gilt, $2.25; *Red-Line Edition*, Portrait and 12 Illustrations, small 4to, $2.50; *Cabinet Edition*, $1.00; *Library Edition*, Portrait and 32 Illustrations, 8vo, $3.50; Christus, *Household Edition*, $1.75; cr. 8vo, full gilt, $2.25; *Cabinet Edition*, $1.00; Prose Works, *Riverside Edition*, 2 vols. cr. 8vo, $3.00; Hyperion, 16mo, $1.50; Kavanagh, 16mo, $1.50; Outre-Mer, 16mo, $1.50; In the Harbor, 16mo, $1.00; Michael Angelo: a Drama, Illustrated, folio, $5.00; Twenty Poems, Illustrated, small 4to, $2.50; Translation of the Divina Commedia of Dante, *Riverside Edition*, 3 vols. cr. 8vo, $4.50; 1 vol. cr. 8vo, $2.50; 3 vols. royal 8vo, $13.50; cr. 8vo, $4.50; Poets and Poetry of Europe, royal 8vo, $5.00; Poems of Places, 31 vols. each $1.00; the set, $25.00.
James Russell Lowell. Poems, *Red-Line Edition*, Portrait, Illustrated, small 4to, $2.50; *Household Edition*, Illustrated, 12mo, $1.75; cr. 8vo, full gilt, $2.25; *Library Edition*, Portrait and 32 Illustrations, 8vo, $3.50; *Cabinet Edition*, $1.00; Fireside Travels, 12mo, $1.50; Among my Books, Series I. and II. 12mo, each $2.00; My Study Windows, 12mo, $2.00; Democracy and other Addresses, 16mo, $1.25; Uncollected Poems.
Thomas Babington Macaulay. Works, 6 vols. 12mo, $20.00.
Mrs. Madison. Memoirs and Letters of Dolly Madison, 16mo, $1.25.
Harriet Martineau. Autobiography, New Edition, 2 vols. 12mo, $4.00; Household Education, 18mo, $1.25.
H. B. McClellan. The Life and Campaigns of Maj.-Gen. J. E. B. Stuart. With Portrait and Maps, 8vo, $3.00.
G. W. Melville. In the Lena Delta, Maps and Illustrations, 8vo, $2.50.

T. C. Mendenhall. A Century of Electricity. 16mo, $1.25.

Owen Meredith. Poems, *Household Edition*, Illustrated, 12mo, $1.75; cr. 8vo, full gilt, $2.25; *Library Edition*, Portrait and 32 Illustrations, 8vo, $3.50; Lucile, *Red-Line Edition*, 8 Illustrations, small 4to, $2.50; *Cabinet Edition*, 8 Illustrations, $1.00.

Olive Thorne Miller. Bird-Ways, 16mo, $1.25.

John Milton. Paradise Lost. *Handy-Volume Edition*. 32mo, $1.00. *Riverside Classic Edition*, 16mo, Illustrated, $1.00.

S. Weir Mitchell. In War Time, 16mo, $1.25; Roland Blake, 16mo, $1.25.

J. W. Mollett. Illustrated Dictionary of Words used in Art and Archæology, small 4to, $5.00.

Montaigne. Complete Works, Portrait, 4 vols. 12mo, $7.50.

William Mountford. Euthanasy, 12mo, $2.00.

T. Mozley. Reminiscences of Oriel College, etc., 2 vols. 16mo, $3.00.

Elisha Mulford. The Nation, 8vo, $2.50; The Republic of God, 8vo, $2.00.

T. T. Munger. On the Threshold, 16mo, $1.00; The Freedom of Faith, 16mo, $1.50; Lamps and Paths, 16mo, $1.00; The Appeal to Life, 16mo, $1.50.

J. A. W. Neander. History of the Christian Religion and Church, with Index volume, 6 vols. 8vo, $20.00; Index, $3.00.

Joseph Neilson. Memories of Rufus Choate, 8vo, $5.00.

Charles Eliot Norton. Notes of Travel in Italy, 16mo, $1.25; Translation of Dante's New Life, royal 8vo, $3.00.

Wm. D. O'Connor. Hamlet's Note-Book, 16mo, $1.00.

G. H. Palmer. Trans. of Homer's Odyssey, 1–12, 8vo, $2.50.

Leighton Parks. His Star in the East. Cr. 8vo, $1.50.

James Parton. Life of Benjamin Franklin, 2 vols. 8vo, $5.00; Life of Thomas Jefferson, 8vo, $2.50; Life of Aaron Burr, 2 vols. 8vo, $5.00; Life of Andrew Jackson, 3 vols. 8vo, $7.50; Life of Horace Greeley, 8vo, $2.50; General Butler in New Orleans, 8vo, $2.50; Humorous Poetry of the English Language, 12mo, $1.75; full gilt, $2.25; Famous Americans of Recent Times, 8vo, $2.50; Life of Voltaire, 2 vols. 8vo, $6.00; The French Parnassus, 12mo, $1.75; crown 8vo, $3.50; Captains of Industry, 16mo, $1.25.

Blaise Pascal. Thoughts, 12mo, $2.25; Letters, 12mo, $2.25.

Elizabeth Stuart Phelps. The Gates Ajar, 16mo, $1.50; Beyond the Gates, 16mo, $1.25; Men, Women, and Ghosts, 16mo, $1.50; Hedged In, 16mo, $1.50; The Silent Partner, 16mo, $1.50; The Story of Avis, 16mo, $1.50; Sealed Orders, and other Stories, 16mo, $1.50; Friends: A Duet, 16mo, $1.25; Doctor Zay, 16mo, $1.25; Songs of the Silent World, 16mo, gilt top, $1.25; An Old Maid's Paradise, 16mo, paper, 50 cents; Burglars in Paradise, 16mo, paper, 50 cents; Madonna of the Tubs, cr. 8vo, Illustrated, $1.50.

Phillips Exeter Lectures: Delivered before the Students of Phillips Exeter Academy, 1885-6. By E. E. HALE, PHILLIPS BROOKS, Presidents McCOSH, PORTER, and others. 12mo, $1.50.

Mrs. S. M. B. Piatt. Selected Poems, 16mo, $1.50.

Carl Ploetz. Epitome of Universal History, 12mo, $3.00.

Antonin Lefevre Pontalis. The Life of John DeWitt, Grand Pensionary of Holland, 2 vols. 8vo, $9.00.

Margaret J. Preston. Colonial Ballads, 16mo, $1.25.

Adelaide A. Procter. Poems, *Cabinet Edition*, $1.00; *Red-Line Edition*, small 4to, $2.50.

Progressive Orthodoxy. 16mo, $1.00.

Sampson Reed. Growth of the Mind, 16mo, $1.00.

C. F. Richardson. Primer of American Literature, 18mo, $.30.

Riverside Aldine Series. Each volume, 16mo, $1.00. First edition, $1.50. 1. Marjorie Daw, etc., by T. B. ALDRICH; 2. My Summer in a Garden, by C. D. WARNER; 3. Fireside Travels, by J. R. LOWELL; 4. The Luck of Roaring Camp, etc., by BRET HARTE; 5, 6. Venetian Life, 2 vols., by W. D. HOWELLS; 7. Wake Robin, by JOHN BURROUGHS; 8, 9. The Biglow Papers, 2 vols., by J. R. LOWELL; 10. Backlog Studies, by C. D. WARNER.

Henry Crabb Robinson. Diary, Reminiscences, etc. cr. 8vo, $2.50.

John C. Ropes. The First Napoleon, with Maps, cr. 8vo, $2.00.

Josiah Royce. Religious Aspect of Philosophy, 12mo, $2.00.

Edgar Evertson Saltus. Balzac, cr. 8vo, $1.25; The Philosophy of Disenchantment, cr. 8vo, $1.25.

John Godfrey Saxe. Poems, *Red-Line Edition*, Illustrated, small 4to, $2.50; *Cabinet Edition*, $1.00; *Household Edition*, Illustrated, 12mo, $1.75; full gilt, cr. 8vo, $2.25.

Sir Walter Scott. Waverley Novels, *Illustrated Library Edition*, 25 vols. 12mo, each $1.00; the set, $25.00; Tales of a Grandfather, 3 vols. 12mo, $4.50; Poems, *Red-Line Edition* Illustrated, small 4to, $2.50; *Cabinet Edition*, $1.00.

W. H. Seward. Works, 5 vols. 8vo, $15.00; Diplomatic History of the War, 8vo, $3.00.

John Campbell Shairp. Culture and Religion, 16mo, $1.25; Poetic Interpretation of Nature, 16mo, $1.25; Studies in Poetry and Philosophy, 16mo, $1.50; Aspects of Poetry, 16mo, $1.50.

William Shakespeare. Works, edited by R. G. White, *Riverside Edition*, 3 vols. cr. 8vo, $7.50; The Same, 6 vols., cr. 8vo, uncut, $10.00; The Blackfriars Shakespeare, per vol. $2.50, *net*. (*In Press.*)

A. P. Sinnett. Esoteric Buddhism, 16mo, $1.25; The Occult World, 16mo, $1.25.

M. C. D. Silsbee. A Half Century in Salem. 16mo, $1.00.

Dr. William Smith. Bible Dictionary, *American Edition*, 4 vols. 8vo, $20.00.

Edmund Clarence Stedman. Poems, *Farringford Edition*, Portrait, 16mo, $2.00; *Household Edition*, Illustrated, 12mo, $1.75; full gilt, cr. 8vo, $2.25; Victorian Poets, 12mo, $2.00; Poets of America, 12mo, $2.25. The set, 3 vols., uniform, 12mo, $6.00; Edgar Allan Poe, an Essay, vellum, 18mo, $1.00.

W. W. Story. Poems, 2 vols. 16mo, $2.50; Fiammetta: A Novel, 16mo, $1.25. Roba di Roma, 2 vols. 16mo, $2.50.

Harriet Beecher Stowe. Novels and Stories, 10 vols. 12mo, uniform, each $1.50; A Dog's Mission, Little Pussy Willow, Queer Little People, Illustrated, small 4to, each $1.25; Uncle Tom's Cabin, 100 Illustrations, 8vo, $3.00; *Library Edition*, Illustrated, 12mo, $2.00; *Popular Edition*, 12mo, $1.00.

Jonathan Swift. Works, *Edition de Luxe*, 19 vols. 8vo, the set, $76.00.

T. P. Taswell-Langmead. English Constitutional History. New Edition, revised, 8vo, $7.50.

Bayard Taylor. Poetical Works, *Household Edition*, 12mo, $1.75; cr. 8vo. full gilt, $2.25; Melodies of Verse, 18mo, vellum, $1.00; Life and Letters, 2 vols. 12mo, $4.00; Dramatic Poems, 12mo, $2.25; *Household Edition*, 12mo, $1.75; Life and Poetical Works, 6 vols. uniform. Including Life, 2 vols.; Faust, 2 vols.; Poems, 1 vol.; Dramatic Poems, 1 vol. The set, cr. 8vo, $12.00.

Alfred Tennyson. Poems, *Household Edition*, Portrait and Illustrations, 12mo, $1.75; full gilt, cr. 8vo, $2.25; *Illustrated Crown Edition*, 2 vols. 8vo, $5.00; *Library Edition*, Portrait and 60 Illustrations, 8vo, $3.50; *Red-Line Edition*, Portrait and Illustrations, small 4to, $2.50; *Cabinet Edition*, $1.00; Complete Works, *Riverside Edition*, 6 vols. cr. 8vo, $6.00.

Celia Thaxter. Among the Isles of Shoals, 18mo, $1.25; Poems, small 4to, $1.50; Drift-Weed, 18mo, $1.50; Poems for Children, Illustrated, small 4to, $1.50; Cruise of the Mystery, Poems, 16mo, $1.00.

Edith M. Thomas. A New Year's Masque and other Poems, 16mo, $1.50; The Round Year, 16mo, $1.25.

Joseph P. Thompson. American Comments on European Questions, 8vo, $3.00.

Henry D. Thoreau. Works, 9 vols. 12mo, each $1.50; the set, $13.50.

George Ticknor. History of Spanish Literature, 3 vols. 8vo, $10.00; Life, Letters, and Journals, Portraits, 2 vols. 12mo, $4.00.

Bradford Torrey. Birds in the Bush, 16mo, $1.25.

Sophus Tromholt. Under the Rays of the Aurora Borealis, Illustrated, 2 vols. $7.50.

Mrs. Schuyler Van Rensselaer. H. H. Richardson and his Works.

Jones Very. Essays and Poems, cr. 8vo, $2.00.

Annie Wall. Story of Sordello, told in Prose, 16mo, $1.00.

Charles Dudley Warner. My Summer in a Garden, *Riverside Aldine Edition*, 16mo, $1.00; *Illustrated Edition*, square 16mo, $1.50; Saunterings, 18mo, $1.25; Backlog Studies, Illustrated, square 16mo, $1.50; *Riverside Aldine Edition*, 16mo, $1.00; Baddeck, and that Sort of Thing, 18mo, $1.00; My Winter on the Nile, cr. 8vo, $2.00; In the Levant, cr. 8vo, $2.00; Being a Boy, Illustrated, square 16mo, $1.50; In the

Wilderness, 18mo, 75 cents; A Roundabout Journey, 12mo, $1.50.

William F. Warren, LL. D. Paradise Found, cr. 8vo, $2.00.

William A. Wheeler. Dictionary of Noted Names of Fiction, 12mo, $2.00.

Edwin P. Whipple. Essays, 6 vols. cr. 8vo, each $1.50.

Richard Grant White. Every-Day English, 12mo, $2.00; Words and their Uses, 12mo, $2.00; England Without and Within, 12mo, $2.00; The Fate of Mansfield Humphreys, 16mo, $1.25; Studies in Shakespeare, 12mo, $1.75.

Mrs. A. D. T. Whitney. Stories, 12 vols. 12mo, each $1.50; Mother Goose for Grown Folks, 12mo, $1.50; Pansies, 16mo, $1.25; Daffodils, 16mo, $1.25; Just How, 16mo, $1.00; Bonnyborough, 12mo, $1.50; Holy Tides, 16mo, 75 cents; Homespun Yarns, 12mo, $1.50.

John Greenleaf Whittier. Poems, *Household Edition*, Illustrated, 12mo, $1.75; full gilt, cr. 8vo, $2.25; *Cambridge Edition*, Portrait, 3 vols. 12mo, $5.25; *Red-Line Edition*, Portrait, Illustrated, small 4to, $2.50; *Cabinet Edition*, $1.00; *Library Edition*, Portrait, 32 Illustrations, 8vo, $3.50; Prose Works, *Cambridge Edition*, 2 vols. 12mo, $3.50; The Bay of Seven Islands, Portrait, 16mo, $1.00; John Woolman's Journal, Introduction by Whittier, $1.50; Child Life in Poetry, selected by Whittier, Illustrated, 12mo, $2.00; Child Life in Prose, 12mo, $2.00; Songs of Three Centuries, selected by Whittier: *Household Edition*, Illustrated, 12mo, $1.75; full gilt, cr. 8vo, $2.25; *Library Edition*, 32 Illustrations, 8vo, $3.50; Text and Verse, 18mo, 75 cents; Poems of Nature, 4to, Illustrated, $6.00; St. Gregory's Guest, etc., 16mo, vellum, $1.00.

Woodrow Wilson. Congressional Government, 16mo, $1.25.

J. A. Wilstach. Translation of Virgil's Works, 2 vols. cr. 8vo, $5.00.

Justin Winsor. Reader's Handbook of American Revolution, 16mo, $1.25.

W. B. Wright. Ancient Cities from the Dawn to the Daylight, 16mo, $1.25.